CUTTING EDGE
BUSINESS
SUCCESS STRATEGIES

CUTTING EDGE
BUSINESS
SUCCESS STRATEGIES

HOW TO "START – SURVIVE – THRIVE" IN THE 21ST CENTURY

CHUCK KEYS

GLOBAL BUSINESS CONSULTANT/COACH

PRIMIX
PUBLISHING
THE WRITE CHOICE

Primix Publishing
East Brunswick Office Evolution
1 Tower Center Boulevard, Ste 1510
East Brunswick, NJ 08816
www.primixpublishing.com
Phone: 1-800-538-5788

Published by Primix Publishing: 01/28/2025

ISBN: 979-8-89194-400-8(sc)
ISBN: 979-8-89194-402-2(hc)
ISBN: 979-8-89194-401-5(e)

Library of Congress Control Number: 2025900112

Any people depicted in stock imagery provided by iStock are models, and such images are being used for illustrative purposes only.

Certain stock imagery © iStock.

DISCLAIMER AND/OR LEGAL NOTICES:
While every attempt has been made to verify information provided in this book, neither the author nor the publisher assumes any responsibility for any errors, omissions or inaccuracies.

Any slights of people or organizations are unintentional. If advice concerning legal or related matters is needed, the services of a qualified professional should be sought. This book is not intended as a source of legal or accounting advice. You should be aware of any laws which govern business transactions or other business practices in your state or province.

The income statements and examples are not intended to represent or guarantee that everyone will achieve the same results. Each individual's success will be determined by his or her desire, dedication, effort, and motivation. There are no guarantees you will duplicate the results stated here, you recognize that any business endeavor has inherent risk for loss of capital.

Any reference to any persons or business, whether living or deceased, existing or defunct, is purely coincidental.

Contents

Book Dedication

I dedicate this book to my daughter Rebecca Lattin with her new husband Brian with all their combined family of 5 children – all my grandchildren: Caleb, Jacob, Morgan, Harper, and Avery and include our Pets "Harold" (my dog, a Terrier) and "Stanley Straight Arrow" (my Siamese Cat). I must also include my former faithful long-time dog "Lucky" the Cocker Spaniel and Rebecca's Cocker Spaniel "Prince" her 17 yr Cocker Spaniel and long-time family member. The pets grew up together with the grandchildren. All our Pets were loved, honored and respected by everyone, family and friends – we are one big loving family. Besides being a Global Business Consultant, I am a writer of books (business and poetry), papers and documents – when I finish my writing sessions, all the pets anxiously wait to be read too, expecting a treat when done – if they are not sleeping!

To my daughter Rebecca, I owe so much to her vitality, energy and passion for perfection. As I was teaching her that the word "can't" was invented for lazy people she was teaching me how to be more positive, fun and active. Yes I played "dolls" with her growing up including the many doll tea parties we had together and when we went shopping, she would make me park the car farthest from the entrance, because she wanted to hold my hand and make me skip with her across the parking lot to the door. She taught me how to enjoy my passion for life with "fun and more laughter". I still laugh with all of my memories. Her motherly instincts are so perfect, I joke with her that she should have been my mother! Today she is still my "bright light."

Growing up with 3 brothers was exciting and competitive. Having a twin brother was an advantage. Twin brother Stephen Keys always stood ready to defend me in in times of need, he was taller and stronger and protective. I remember in summer camp, I was always crying at night, afraid of everything. He would welcome me in his bed to keep me secure and content. If challenged in battle at school, he stood up for me. As we aged, he still presented himself at the right times. When I became a Police Officer, friends and family were in shock, but Stephen had trained me well. His attention growing up made me feel admiration and respect for him. I value Stephen greatl. I also have Dr. Diane Kulick MD, my sister-in-law and my current Medical Champion added another dimension to Stephen. I owe their constant care and positive input to my success.

We live in turbulent times of rapid change often expressed in anger and intolerance with up and down reactive growth, standards that fluctuate dramatically and lack reliability, an environment that reacts negatively to pollution, enormous population shifts/migrations to avoid hunger with political uncertainty. We experienced Covid killing millions of our global population, that still lingers and threatens all security in our planet, fires, floods, hurricanes that destroy entire cities, villages, with the destruction of our homes, businesses, schools, religious house of prayers, factories, seashores, including historical sites – all wiped away almost magically.

I wrote this book to help those in business expand their horizons and grow, to have   a reference, a handy portable reference guide of tried, true, tested and proven successful business strategies. I will shortly have available a series of video recorded discussions to be available on my web site to expand this books content to include specific real life applications, suggestions, how to create opportunities to further learn and expand, and again to exceed ones expectations.   In a way, this book is also dedicated to you, the reader, with your efforts to expand and grow.

Writing this book was a work of joy and love. When I started in business, I had no one to help or to go to for assistance. I promised myself that I would not let others suffer as I did, so alone. I have much to teach, to pass on to those younger and hungry enough to learn for success. And I hope that those I teach pass on their knowledge and experience to the many others in need.

Now this book, written to teach the art of starting, managing and expanding your business to exceed your expectations, captures your success. So, go for it!

Thank you,
Chuck Keys
Dated: 01/16/2025

Introduction

By opening this book you have already taken an important step towards increasing the success of your business. Congratulations in your quest to enhance your business and marketing skills.

My experience is drawn from many different life and business experiences. Starting my early professional life as a Detroit Police Officer to now where I am proudly and currently an Author, Public Speaker, President/CEO of Keys2Business, LLC Business Coaching/Consulting, a Medical Records Company, Financial Services and Insurance Company and an Energy Brokerage Firm. In addition I have a life-time that entails a political career, published poetry book, social and community activism. The strategies I talk about in this book are still in place at all of these successful companies.

I believe the first two chapters are as important as the remaining. The strategies in this book - when implemented with strategy and care - are guaranteed to make you more money with less effort. These are strategies that have helped businesses just like yours make hundreds of thousands of dollars - including your competitors.

As an avid reader, I open myself up to more and more learning experiences. My many years have taught me to take advantage of opportunities as they appear – that "focus and preparation" are essential; as stated in the words of noted Author, Mary Stewart "the Gods only go with you if you put yourself in their path – and that takes courage." I remember in my early learning that life's fulfillments entails "Thought,

Speech & Action" – that one can't happen without the other two; and without all three – we stagnate. And that's not acceptable.

This is the reason I have dedicated my life to Business Coaching and Consulting. Since starting my company to provide direction for small business operators, I have been literally overwhelmed with the demand for marketing, structure, accountability and for the need to have small business operators surrounding themselves with someone that cares and to provide a proper and profitable third party perspective.

As you follow the book and read the principles to follow, remember it does not matter what industry nor type of business you operate (I've worked with many). What matters is that you grasp the heart of the principles, the underlying lessons and strategies, that can help grow any operation in any category of business imaginable.

The best time to start is NOW, not tomorrow, not next week or next year.

Yours in success,

Chuck Keys

PS. If you would like to arrange a meeting to get a profitable third party perspective on your business, please send an email to Chuck@ Keys2Business.com and we will gladly point you in the right direction.

For a Free Test Drive of all my best tips, tricks and marketing resources visit www.Keys2BusinessMarketing.com

1

Creating a Powerful Offer

I'm not going to beat around the bush on this one:

> *Your offer is the granite foundation of your marketing campaign.*

Get it right, and everything else will fall into place. Your headline will grab readers, your copy will sing, your ad layout will hardly matter, and you will have customers running to your door.

Get it wrong, and even the best looking, best-written campaign will sink like the Titanic.

A powerful offer is an irresistible offer. It's an offer that gets your audience frothing at the mouth and clamoring over each other all the way to your door. An offer that makes your readers pick up the phone and open their wallets.

Irresistible offers make your potential customers think, "I'd be crazy not to take him up on that," or "An offer like this doesn't come around very often." They instill a sense of emotion, of desire, and ultimately, urgency.

1

Make it easy for customers to purchase from you the first time, and spend your time keeping them coming back.

I'll say it again: **get it right, and everything else will fall into place.**

The Crux of Your Marketing Campaign

As you work your way through this program, you will find that nearly every chapter discusses the importance of a powerful offer as related to your marketing strategy or promotional campaign.

There's a reason for this. The powerful offer is more often than not the reason a customer will open their wallets. It is how you generate leads, and then convert them into loyal customers. The more dramatic, unbelievable, and valuable the offer is the more dramatic and unbelievable the response will be.

Many companies spend thousands of dollars on impressive marketing campaigns in glossy magazines and big city newspapers. They send massive direct mail campaigns on a regular basis; yet don't receive an impressive or massive response rate.

These companies do not yet understand that simply providing information on their company and the benefits of their product is not enough to get customers to act. There is no reason to pick up the phone or visit the store, *right now.*

Your powerful, irresistible offer can:
- Increase leads
- Drive traffic to your website or business
- Move old product
- Convert leads into customers
- Build your customer database

What Makes a Powerful Offer?

A powerful offer is one that makes the most people respond, and take action. It gets people running to spend money on your product or service.

Powerful offers nearly always have an element of *urgency* and of *scarcity*. They give your audience a reason to act immediately, instead of put it off until a later date.

Urgency relates to time. The offer is only available until a certain date, during a certain period of the day, or if you act within a few hours of seeing the ad. The customer needs to act now to take advantage of the offer.

Scarcity related to quantity. There are only a certain number of customers who will be able to take advantage of the offer. There may be a limited number of spaces, a limited number of products, or simply a limited number of people the business will provide the offer to. Again, this requires that customer acts immediately to reap the high value for low cost.

Powerful offers also:

Offer great value. Customers perceive the offer as having great value – more than a single product on its own, or the product at its regular price. It is clear that the offer takes the reader's needs and wants into consideration.

Make sense to the reader. They are simple and easy to understand if read quickly. Avoid percentages – use half off or 2 for 1 instead of 50% off. There are no "catches" or requirements; no fine print.

Seem logical. The offer doesn't come out of thin air. There is a logical reason behind it – a holiday, end of season, anniversary celebration, or new product. People can get suspicious of offers that seem "too good to be true" and have no apparent purpose.

Provide a premium. The offer provides something extra to the customer, like a free gift, or free product or service. They feel they are getting something extra for no extra cost. Premiums are perceived to have more value than discounts.

Remember that when your target market reads your offer, they will be asking the following questions:

1. What are you offering me?
2. What's in it for me?
3. What makes me sure I can believe you?
4. How much do I have to pay for it?

The Most Powerful Types of Offers

Decide what kind of offer will most effectively achieve your objectives. Are you trying to generate leads, convert customers, build a database, move old product off the shelves, or increase sales?

Consider what type of offer will be of most value to your ideal customers – what offer will make them act quickly.

Free Offer

This type of offer asks customers to act immediately in exchange for something free. This is a good strategy to use to build a customer database or mailing list. Offer a free consultation, free consumer report, or other item of low cost to you but of high perceived value.

You can also advertise the value of the item you are offering for free. For example, act now and you'll receive a free consultation, worth $75 dollars. This will dramatically increase your lead generation, and allow you to focus on conversion when the customer comes through the door or picks up the phone.

The Value Added Offer

Add additional services or products that cost you very little, and combine them with other items to increase their attractiveness. This increases the perception of value in the customer's mind, which will justify increasing the price of a product or service without incurring extra hard costs to your business.

Package Offer

Package your products or services together in a logical way to increase the perceived value as a whole. Discount the value of the package by a small margin, and position it as a "start-up kit" or "special package." By packaging goods of mixed values, you will be able to close more high-value sales. For example: including a free desk-jet printer with every computer purchase.

Premium Offer

Offer a bonus product or service with the purchase of another. This strategy will serve your bottom line much better than discounting. This includes 2 for 1 offers, offers that include free gifts, and in-store credit with purchases over a specific dollar amount.

Urgency Offer

As I mentioned above, offers that include an element of urgency enjoy a better response rate, as there is a reason for your customers to act immediately. Give the offer a deadline or limit the number of spots available.

Guarantee Offer

Offer to take the risk of making a purchase away from your customers. Guarantee the performance or results of your product or service, and offer to compensate the customer with their money back if they are not satisfied. This will help overcome any fear or reservations about your product, and make it more likely for your leads to become customers.

Create Your Powerful Offer

1. Pick a single product or service.

Focus on only one product or service – or one product or service *type* – at a time. This will keep your offer clear, simple, and easy to understand. This can be an area of your business you wish to grow, or old product that you need to move off the shelves.

2. Decide what you want your customers to do.

What are you looking to achieve from your offer? If it is to generate more leads, then you'll need your customer to contact you. If it is to quickly sell old product, you'll need your customer to come into the store and buy it. Do you want them to visit your website? Sign up for your newsletter? How long do they have to act? Be clear about your call to action, and state it clearly in your offer.

3. Dream up the biggest, best offer.

First, think of the biggest, best things you could offer your customers – regardless of cost and ability. Don't limit yourself to a single type of offer, combine several types of offers to increase value. Offer a premium, plus a guarantee, with a package offer. Then take a look at what you've created, and make the necessary changes so it is realistic.

4. Run the numbers.

Finally, make sure the offer will leave you with some profit – or at least allow you to break even. You don't want to publish an outrageous offer that will generate a tremendous number of leads, but leave you broke. Remember that each customer has an acquisition cost, as well as a lifetime value. The amount of their first purchase may allow you to break even, but the amount of their subsequent purchases may make you a lovely profit.

2

Profiting from Internet Marketing

Is your business online? If not, it should be.

The internet is today's primary consumer research tool. If your business does not have an online presence, it is harder for customers to find and choose your business over the competition. With over 73% of North Americans online, it is no wonder that individuals and businesses in all industries are looking to the internet to enhance their marketing strategies.

Luckily, it has never been easier to establish and maintain a comprehensive online presence. Internet marketing, also referred to as online marketing, online advertising or e-marketing, is the fastest growing medium for marketing.

But it is not just company websites that users are viewing. Blogs, consumer reviews, chat rooms and a variety of social media are growing rapidly in popularity.

The internet is a very powerful tool for businesses if used strategically and effectively. It can be a cost saving alternative to traditional marketing approaches, and may be the most effective way to communicate with your target consumer.

A major advantage of the internet is that you are always open. Users can access your business 24 hours a day, 7 days a week, and depending on your business and the purpose of the website, visitors can also purchase goods at any time.

Internet Marketing for Everyone

The internet is a great way to create product and brand awareness, develop relationships with consumers and share and exchange information. You can't afford not be taking advantage of online marketing opportunities because your competition is likely already there.

Internet marketing can take on many different forms. By creating maintaining a website for your business, you are reaching out to a new consumer base. You can have full control over the messaging that users are receiving and has a global reach.

Internet marketing can be very cost effective. If you have a strong email database of your customers, an e-newsletter may be cheaper and more effective than post mail. You can deliver time sensitive materials immediately and can update your subscribers instantaneously.

Top 10 Websites (Globally)

1. Yahoo.com
2. Google.com
3. You Tube
4. Windows Live
5. Facebook
6. MSN.com
7. MySpace
8. Wikipedia
9. Blogger.com
10. Yahoo Japan

You will notice that half of these websites are search engines. An increasing number of consumers are first researching products, services and companies online, whether it be to compare products, complete a sale, or look for a future employer. Most people in the 18-35 age group obtain all of their information online—including news, weather, product research, etc. The remaining sites are interactive sites where users can upload information for social networking, or information sharing.

Internet Marketing Strategies

Internet marketing – like all other elements of your marketing campaign – needs to have clear goals and objectives. Creating brand and product awareness will not happen overnight so it is important to budget accordingly, ensuring there is money set aside for maintenance of the website and analytics.

Be flexible with ideas and options—do your research first, try out different options, then test and measure the results. Metrics and evaluations can be updated almost immediately and should be monitored regularly. By keeping an eye out for what online marketing strategies are working and which are not, it will be easier to create a balanced portfolio of marketing techniques. You might find that in certain geographical areas, certain marketing strategies are more effective than others.

This list is by no means the full extent of options available for marketing online, but it is a good place to start when deciding which options are best suited to your company.

Create a website

The primary use for the internet is information seeking, so you should provide consumers with information about your company first hand. You have more control over your branding and messaging and can also collect visitor information to determine what types of internet users are accessing your website.

Search Engine Optimization

Since search engines comprise 50% of the most visited sites globally, you can go through your website to make it more search engine friendly with the aim to increase your organic search listing. An organic search listing refers to listings in search engine results that appear in order or relevance to the entered search terms.

You may wish to repeat key words multiple times throughout your website and write the copy on your site not only with the end reader in mind, but also search engines.

Remember when you design your website that any text that appears in Flash format is not recognized by search engines. If your entire website is built on a Flash platform, then you will have a poor organic search listing.

Price Per Click Advertising

If you find that visitors access your website after searching for it first on a search engine, then it may be beneficial to advertise on these websites and bid on keywords associated with your company.

These advertisements will appear at the top of the page or along the left side of the search results on a search engine. You can have control over the specific geographic area you wish to target, set a monthly budget and have the option on only being charged when a user clicks on your link.

Online Directories

Listing your business in an online directory can be an inexpensive and effective online marketing strategy.

However, you need to be able to distinguish your company from the plethora of competitors that may exist. Likely, you will need to complement this strategy with other brand awareness campaigns.

Online Ads (i.e. banner ads on other websites)

These advertisements can have positive or negative effects based on the reputation and consumer perception of the website on which you are advertising. These ads should be treated similar to print ads you may place in local newspapers or other publications.

Online Videos

With the growing popularity of sites such as You Tube, it is evident that people love researching online and being able to find video clips of the information they are seeking. Depending on your small business, you may want to upload informational videos or tutorials about your products or services.

Blogging

Blogging can be a fun and interactive way to communicate with users. A blog is traditionally a website maintained by an individual user that has regular entries, similar to a diary. These entries can be commentary, descriptions of events, pictures, videos, and more. Companies can use blogging as a way to keep users updated on current information and allow them to post comments on your blog. If blogging is something you wish to invest in, make sure that it is regularly updated and monitored.

Top 10 Mistakes to Avoid

Failure to measure ROI

Which metrics are you using? Are your visitors actually motivated to purchase or sign up? If the benefits of your online campaign are not greater than the costs incurred, then you may wish to re-evaluate your strategy.

Poor Web Design

This can leave a poor impression of your company on the visitor. A poor design could result in frustration on the visitors' part if they are not able to easily find what they went on your site to search for and also does not build trust. If consumers do not trust your company or your website, you will not be able to complete the sale and develop a longer relationship with that customer. You also need to include privacy protection and security when building trust.

This also includes ensuring all information on the website is current and having customer service available if users are experiencing difficulty or cannot find the information they are seeking. This could be as simple as providing a 'Contact Us' email or phone number for support.

Becoming locked into an advertising strategy early

Remember your marketing mix when creating a marketing strategy and avoid putting all of your eggs in one basket. Online marketing is a very valuable tool, but depending on your business and your target markets, other marketing campaigns may be the best option for you. Especially if this is your first time making a significant investment into your online sector, you want to remain flexible and able to adapt your strategy based off feedback received by researching and analyzing different options.

Acting without researching

Similar to becoming locked into an advertising strategy early, this mistake implies not dutifully testing and researching different online marketing options. For example, if your target consumer is aged 65+ and you are spending all of your marketing efforts into creating a blogging website (where the average ages of bloggers are 18-35), then you are likely not going to have a successful campaign.

Assuming more visitors means more sales

You have to go back to your original goals and the purpose of your company. More visitors may not mean more sales if your website is used primarily for information and consumers purchase their products elsewhere. This is also vice versa. You could have an increase in sales without an increase in unique visitors if your current consumer base is very loyal and willing to spend lots of money.

Often people will collect information online about products they wish to purchase because it is easier to compare options, but they purchase in person. Even though shopping online is becoming quite popular, people still prefer to see and feel the physical product before purchasing.

Failing to follow up with customers that purchase

Return sales can account for up to 60% of total revenue. It's no wonder that organizations are always trying to maintain loyal customers and may have customer relationship management systems in place. It is easier to get a happy customer to purchase again than it is to get a new customer to purchase once.

Not incorporating online marketing into the business plan

By ensuring that your online marketing plan is fully integrated and accurately represents your organization's overall goals and objectives, the business plan will be more comprehensive and encompassing.

Trying to discover your own best practices

It is very beneficial to use trial and error to determine the best online strategy from your company, but do not be afraid to do your research and learn from what other have already figured out. There will be many cases where someone was in a very similar position as you and they may have some suggestions and secrets that they wish to share. Researching in advance can save a great deal of time and money.

Spending too much too fast

Although it may be cheaper than traditional marketing approaches, internet marketing does have its costs. You have to consider the software and hardware designs, maintenance, distribution, supply chain management, and the time that will be required. You don't want to spend your entire marketing budget all at once.

Getting distracted by metrics that are not relevant

As discussed in the following section, there are endless reports and measurables that you can analyze to determine the effectiveness of your campaign. You will need to establish which measurables are actually relevant to your marketing.

Testing and Measuring Online

As with any element of your marketing campaign, you will need to track your results and measure them against your investment. Otherwise, how will you know if your online marketing is successful?

These results - or metrics – need to be recorded and analyzed as to how they impact your overall return on investment.

Some examples of metrics are:

- New account setups
- Conversion rates
- Page stickiness
- Contact us form completion

Due to the popularity in online marketing and the importance of having a strong web presence, companies have demanded more sophisticated tracking tools and metrics for their online activities. It can be very difficult to not only know what to measure, but also HOW to measure.

Thankfully, it is easier than ever to get the information you need with the many types of software and services available, including Google Analytics, which are free and relatively accurate.

8 Metrics to Track

The following are the key measurables to watch for when testing and measuring your internet marketing efforts:

Conversions

How many leads has your online presence generated, and of those leads, how many were turned into sales? Ultimately, your campaign needs to have a positive impact on your business.

Regardless of the specific purpose of the campaign – from lead generation and service sign-up, to blog entries – you need to know how many customers are taking the desired action in response to your efforts. Your tracking tool will be able to provide you with this information

Spend

If you are not making a profit – or at least breaking even – from your internet marketing efforts, then you need to change your strategy. Redistribute your financial resources and reconsider your motives and objectives for your online campaign.

An easy way to do this analysis is to divide your total spend by conversions. This could also be broken down by product. You could also use tracking tool and view reports on the 'per visit value of every click,' from every type of source. Your sources can include organic/ search engine referrals, direct visit (i.e. person typed your web address into their address bar), or email/newsletter.

Attention

You need to keep a close eye on how much attention you are getting on your website. One of the best ways to analyze this would be to compare unique visitors to page views per visit to time on site. How many people are visiting, how many pages they are viewing, what pages they are viewing, and how much time they are spending on the site.

A unique visitor is any one person who visits the website in a given amount of time. For example, if Evelyn visits her online banking website daily for an entire month, over that one month period, she is considered to be one unique visitor (not 30 visitors).

You may also want to incorporate referring source as well – the places online that refer customers to your website. You'll be able to determine what referring sources offer the 'best' visitors.

Top Referrals

Know who is doing the best job of referring clients to your website – and note how they are doing this. Is it the prominence of the link? Positioning? Reputation of the referring company?

Understanding where the majority of your visitors are coming from will allow you focus on those types of sources when you increase your referral sites. They also allow you to gain a better understanding of your online market – and target audience.

Bounce Rate

The bounce rate is the number of people who visit the homepage of your website, but do not visit other pages. If you have a high bounce rate, you either have all the necessary information on your homepage, or you are not giving your customers a reason to click further.

In Google Analytics, view the 'content' or 'pages' report and view the column stating bounce rate.

Errors

It is very important to track the errors that visitors receive while trying to access or view your website. For example, if someone links to your website, but makes a spelling error in typing the link, your users will see an error page in their browser, and will not ultimately make it to your website.

You can also receive reports on errors that customer's make when trying to type in your website address in their browser. You may wish to buy the domains with common spelling mistakes, and link those addresses to you true homepage. This will increase overall traffic and potential conversions.

Onsite Search Terms

If you have a 'search website' function on your website, it is useful to monitor which terms users are most frequently searching. This can provide valuable insight into the user friendliness of your site and your website's navigation system. This information will be included in the traffic reporting tool.

Bailout Rates

If you provide users with the option to purchase something on your website (i.e. shopping cart), then you can track where along the purchasing process people decided not to go through with the sale.

This could be at the first step of receiving the order summary and total, or further when stating shipping options. By obtaining this information, a company can reorganize or revamp their website to make the sales process more fluid and possibly encourage more purchases.

Here are the three main questions you should be asking yourself when evaluating your website presence:

- Who visits my website?
- Where do visitors come from?
- Which pages are viewed?

3

How to Use Advertising
for Immediate Profits

Why do you advertise?

Seems like a silly question, doesn't it? Placing ads in newspapers and on the radio seems like a no-brainer way of growing or maintaining your business. You let a group of people know where your business is and what you sell, and you'll always have customers dropping by, right?

Sure, it's a little more complicated than that. There's your powerful offer, your strong guarantee, the placement of your headline, and how you structure your body copy.

But what I'm really trying to drill down to is *why* you chose to place *that* ad. What is the specific purpose for each advertisement you send out into the world?

Without a solid purpose – or strategy – behind each and every advertisement, it is impossible to measure what is and is not working. If you placed an ad offering 2 for 1 shampoo one week, and sales for conditioner skyrocketed, would you consider your ad successful? Absolutely not. Sales might have gone up, but the reason you placed the ad was to speed sales on shampoo, which didn't happen.

The point is that each and every advertising dollar should be spent with purpose, focused on a desired outcome and relevant to the big picture. Advertising is expensive! What's the point, unless you're making your money back and then some?

Types of Advertising

There are endless options when it comes to choosing which media to place your advertisements with. The media is a broad and complicated industry, with highly segmented readership.

This can help and hurt your advertising efforts. You have access to highly targeted audiences, but you also may spend a great deal of money on expensive advertising that your target market doesn't go near.

Here are the major types of media advertising:

Print

Print is the most common form of advertising. Ad production is relatively easy and straightforward, and placement is less expensive than broadcast advertising. We'll be focusing on this form of advertising in detail later in the chapter.

Types of print media:
Newspapers – daily and weekly
Magazines
Trade Journals
Newsletters

Radio

Radio advertising reaches a broad audience within a geographic area. This form of advertising can be highly profitable for some businesses, and utterly useless for others. Always consider if there is a simpler, cheaper way of getting your message to your target audience.

Key points to consider for radio advertising:

Use of sounds, voices, tones
Length
Gaining listener's attention
Call to action

Television

Television advertising is largely out of reach for most small business budgets. Creating, developing, and producing TV spots is a costly endeavor, and does not always generate an acceptable return on investment.

This form of advertising generally reaches a broad audience, depending on the timeslot the ad spot airs. Typically, the most expensive airspace is during the region's most popular 6 o'clock news program, or prime time (6pm to 10pm) television line-up.

There are some cost-effective alternatives to TV advertising that you can implement online. You could create a promotional video for your company, and post it on your website and YouTube, or Facebook, or play it in your store. Be creative with your ad budget when it comes to broadcast media.

Online

Online advertising has emerged as an effective tool for your marketing efforts. Internet usage has dramatically increased, and usage patterns have become easier to identify. This form of advertising also allows you to reach a highly qualified audience with minimal investment in ad creation.

Places to advertise online:

Facebook
Google Adwords
Online media (online newspapers and broadcast stations)

Craigslist
Banner ads on complementary websites

Classified

Classified advertising is one of the most highly targeted and cost-effective choices you can make in your overall strategy. People who read classifieds have typically made a decision to buy something, and are looking for places to do so. This is also a great way to test your headlines, offer, and guarantee before you invest in higher-priced advertising.

Classified ad types:

Daily and weekly newspapers
Online
Trade journals

Specific tips for effective classified ads:

- Pick a format for your ad within the specifications of the publication. Will it look like a print display ad? A semi-display ad? A classic line ad? This will affect how you structure your message.

- Choose the category – or two – that best fit with what you have to offer. If two apply, place an ad in both and measure which category generated more leads.

- Grab the attention of your reader with a killer headline, then list benefits, make an irresistible offer, and offer a strong guarantee. Keep the layout simple and ensure the font size is easy to read.

- Notice how other companies are creating their ads, and do something to stand out. The classifieds page is typically cluttered and full of text, so you will need to distinguish your business in some way.

- Use standard abbreviations when creating line ads to maintain consistency. Ask the ad department for a list of abbreviations they typically use.

Niche

Niche advertising can take any of the forms discussed above. The advantage of niche advertising is the super segmentation of each outlet's audience. Typically, there is a very small market in each niche, and a single publication that caters to it. This is very effective for companies who have no need for broad market advertising in traditional or mainstream publications.

Types of niche advertising:

Trade journals
Alternative media
Online blogs
Internal communications – newsletters, etc.

Your Advertising Strategy

Develop a strategy that is purpose driven.

Know exactly why you are choosing advertising, as well as the objective of each and every ad. Compare the benefits of advertising to other promotional strategies like media relations, direct mail, referral strategies and customer loyalty programs.

Some common objectives for advertising strategies include:

- Generate qualified leads

- Increase sales
- Promote new products or services
- Position products or services
- Increase business awareness
- Maintain business awareness
- Complement existing promotional strategies

These objectives will dictate where you advertise, how big each of your advertisements is, and how often you advertise in each outlet.

Find your target audience.

Before you do *anything*, get a solid handle on who your target market is, and each of the segments within it. Think about demographic factors like age, sex, location and occupation, as well as behavioral factors like spending motivations and habits.

The composition of your target audience will be the deciding factor when choosing which media to advertise with, and what to say in each of the advertisements.

Decide on a frequency.

The frequency of your advertising campaign will depend on a number of factors, including budget, purpose, outlet, results, and timing. You may wish to publish a weekly ad that includes a coupon in your local paper. Or, you may only need to advertise a few times a year, just before your peak seasons.

Establish an advertising schedule for the year, or at least each quarter, and plan each advertisement in advance. This will ensure you are not scrambling to place an ad at the last minute, and that each ad is part of an overall proactive strategy instead of a reactive one.

Choose your outlets.

Decide where you are going to advertise and how often in each outlet. You may wish to choose a variety of media to reach several target audiences, or just a large daily newspaper where the most number of people will see it.

It is a good idea when you are starting a new campaign to test its effectiveness in smaller, less expensive publications. Based on the results, you can make changes to the ad and place it in the more expensive outlets.

Remember that although budget is a large factor when deciding on advertising mediums, it is entirely possible to implement a successful ad campaign with minimal cost investment. The key is to make sure that each dollar you spend is carefully thought through – and that your ads are placed in publications that will reach your ideal customers.

Maximize your ad spend with bulk purchases.

If you plan to advertise in a specific publication several times in a given time period, you will benefit from a meeting with the sales representative to review your needs. Often, media outlets will offer discounted rates for multiple placements.

Remember that one company may own several media outlets – including TV, radio, and online media. Ask your sales rep for other discount opportunities when advertising within the ownership group.

Remember to test and measure

How will you know if your campaign is successful if you don't test and measure the results? The only true mistake you can make in advertising is neglecting to track and analyze the results each ad generates.

Get in the habit of keeping a copy of each ad, and record all the details of the placement, including publication, cost, date, response rate, and conversion rate. Many publications will mail you a clipping of your advertisement with your account statement, but don't rely on this as a clipping service.

Evaluate the effectiveness of each ad you place, and learn from what isn't working. If you are advertising in several outlets, make sure asking customers where they saw your ad is part of your incoming phone script and sales script. You will need to monitor not only what types of ads work the best, but also where the ads generate the highest response.

Creating Your Advertisement

You don't need to rely on professional copywriting or design assistance when crafting advertisements from your business. Spend your time and resources on what you are saying, ensure the 'how you say it' is clear, clean, and easy to read.

Ad copy

Headlines
- Take at least half of the time you spend creating your ad, and focus on the headline. Your headline will be the difference between your ad getting read – or not. Boldface your headlines for impact.

- You have about five seconds to grab the reader's attention, so create a headline that sparks curiosity, communicates benefits, or states something unbelievable.

Sub Headlines
- The purpose of your sub headline is to elaborate on your headline, and convince the audience to read the body copy. All the rules of headline writing apply. If you did not mention benefits in your headline, do it in your sub headline. Clearly tell the reader what is "in it for them," and get them reading on.

Body Copy
- Choose your words wisely – you don't have room for lengthy paragraphs. Use bullet points to convey benefits wherever

possible, and keep your sentences short. You typically only have about 45 words to convince the customer to keep reading.

- Remember to always include your contact information – phone number and website address at the very least. This seems obvious, but can be forgotten in the design process.

Ad Layout

Size

- Choose your ad size based on the purpose of the ad, and the budget you have available. Larger ads are more expensive, but you do need enough space to communicate your key messages to the audience.

- If you place regular ads to maintain a presence in the local paper, you likely don't need full pages of space. Alternately, if you are launching a new product or service, or having a blowout sale, you will want to buy more space to increase the potential impact.

Graphics

- Graphics should comprise about 25% of your total ad space, and more if you have a small amount of copy. Avoid drawings and clip art. Photographs will generate a better response. Don't underestimate the importance of white space. Give the reader space to "rest" their eyes between headlines and body copy paragraphs.

Font

- Choose clean fonts that are easy to read. Times New Roman and Arial are effective, simple choices. If you use two fonts in your advertisement, make sure you do not combine serif and sans serif fonts, and you keep consistency amongst headers and body copy.

- Ensure that none of your copy is smaller than 9pt. Your audience won't take the time or spend the effort to read tiny copy.

4

Systemizing Your Business and Developing Effective Processes

One of the biggest mistakes a business owner can make is to create a company that is dependent on the owner's involvement for the success of its daily operations. This is called working "in" your business. You're writing basic sales letters, licking stamps, and guiding staff step-by-step through each task.

There are a number of problems with this approach. One is redundancy. You're paying your staff to carry out tasks that you eventually complete. The second is poor time management. You're spending your day – at your high hourly rate – on tasks as they arise, leaving little room for the tasks you need to be focused on.

However, the biggest issue I have with this approach is that countless intelligent business owners are spending the majority of their time operating their business, instead of *growing* it.

A good test of this is to ask yourself, what would happen if you took off to a hot sunny destination for three weeks and left your cell phone, PDA and laptop at home. Would your business be able to continue operating?

If you said no, then this chapter is for you.

Systemizing your business is about putting policies and procedures in place to make your business operations run smoother – and more importantly – without your constant involvement. With your newfound free time, **you will be able to focus your efforts on the bigger picture: strategically growing your business.**

Why Systemize?

For most small business owners, systems simply mean freedom from the day-to-day functioning of their organization. The company runs smoothly, makes a profit, and provides a high level of service – regardless of the owner's involvement.

Systemizing your business is also a healthy way to plan for the future. You're not going to be working forever – what happens when you retire? How will you transition your business to new ownership or management? How will you take that vacation you've been dreaming of?

Businesses that function without their ownership are also highly valuable to investors. Systemizing your business can position it in a favorable light for purchase, and merit a high price tag.

A system is any process, policy, or procedure that consistently achieves the same result, regardless of who is completing the task.

Any task that is performed in your business more than once can be systemized. Ideally, the tasks that are completed on a cyclical basis – daily, weekly, monthly, and quarterly – should be systemized so much so that anyone can perform them.

Systems can take many forms – from manuals and instruction sheets, to signs, banners, and audio or video recordings. They don't have to be elaborate or extensive, just provide enough information in step-by-step form to guide the person performing the task.

Benefits of Business Systems

There are unlimited benefits available to you and your business through systemization. The more systems you can successfully implement, the more benefits you'll see.

- Better cost management
- Improved time management
- Clearer expectations of staff
- More effective staff training and orientation
- Increased productivity (and potentially profits)
- Happier customers (consistent service)
- Maximized conversion rates
- Increased staff respect for your time
- Increased level of individual initiative
- Greater focus on long-term business growth

Taking Stock of Your Existing Systems

The first step in systemizing your business is taking a long look at the existing systems (if any) in your business. At this point, you can look for any systems that have simply emerged as "the way we do things here."

How do your staff answer the phone? What is the process customers go through when dealing with your business? How are employees hired? Trained? How is performance Reviewed and rewarded?

Some of your systems may be highly effective, and not require any changes. Others may be ineffective and require some reworking. If you have previously established some systems, now is a good time to check-in and evaluate how well they are functioning.

Use the following chart to record what systems currently exist in your business.

Existing Systems	
Administration	
Financials	
Communication	
Customer Relations	
Employees	
Marketing	
Data	

Seven Areas to Systemize

There is no doubt that system creation – especially when none exist to begin with – is a daunting and time-consuming task. For many businesses, it can be difficult to determine where to start to make the best use of their time from the onset.

Here are seven main areas of your business you can to systemize. Begin with one area, and move to the other areas as you are ready. Alternately, start with one or two systems within each area, and evaluate how those new systems affect your business. Each business will require its own unique set of systems.

1. Administration

This is an important area of your business to systemize because administrative roles tend to see a high turnover. A series of systems will reduce training time, and keep you from explaining how the phones are to be answered each time a new receptionist joins your team.

Administrative Systems	
Opening and closing procedures	Filing and paper management
Phone greeting	Workflow
Mail processing	Document production
Sending couriers	Inventory management
Office maintenance (watering plants,	Order processing
emptying recycle bins, etc.)	Making orders

2. Financials

This is one area of systems that you will need to keep a close eye on – but that doesn't mean you have to do the work yourself. Financial management systems are everything from tracking credit card purchases to invoicing clients and following up on overdue accounts.

These systems will help to prevent employee theft, and allow you to always have a clear picture of your numbers. It will allow you to control purchasing, and ensure that each decision is signed-off on.

Financial Systems	
Purchasing	Profit / loss statements
Credit card purchase tracking	Invoicing
Accounts payable	Daily cash out
Accounts receivable	Petty cash
Bank deposits	Employee expenses
Cutting checks	Payroll
Tax payments	Commission payments

3. Communications

The area of communication is essential and time consuming for any business. Fax cover letters, sales letters, internal memos, reports, and newsletters are items that need to be created regularly by different people in your organization.

Most of the time, these communications aren't much different from one to the next, yet each are created from scratch by a different person. There is a huge opportunity for systemization in this area of your business. Systemized communication ensures consistency and company differentiation.

Communication Systems	
Internal memo template	Newsletter template
Fax cover template	Sales letter template(s)
Letterhead template	Meeting minutes template
Team meeting agenda	Report template
Sending faxes	Internal meetings
Internal emails	Scheduling

4. Customer Relations

Another important area for systemization is customer relations. This includes everything the customer sees or touches in your company, as well as any interaction they might have with you or your staff members.

Establishing a customer relations system will also ensure that new staff members understand how customers are handled in *your* business. It will allow you to maintain a high level of customer service, without constantly reminding staff of your policies. It will also ensure that the success of your customer relations and retention does not hinge on you or any other individual salesperson.

Customer Relations Systems	
Incoming phone call script	Sales process
Outgoing phone call script	Sales script
Customer service standards	Newsletter templates
Customer retention strategy	Ongoing customer
Customer communications templates	communication strategy
	Customer liaison policy

5. Employees

Create systems in your business for hiring, training, and developing your employees. This will establish clear expectations for the employee, and streamline time consuming activities like recruitment.

Employees with clear expectations who work within clear structures are happier and more productive. They are motivated to achieve 'A' when they know they will receive 'B' if they do. Establishing a clear training manual will also save you and your staff the time and hassle of training each new staff member on the fly.

Employee Systems	
Employee recruitment	Staff uniforms or dress code
Employee retention	Employee training
Incentive and rewards program	Ongoing training and
Regular employee reviews	professional development
Employee feedback structure	Job descriptions and role profiles

6. Marketing

This is likely an area in which you spend a large part of your time. You focus on generating new leads and getting more people to call you or walk through your doors. These efforts can be systemized and delegated to other staff members.

Use the information in this program to create simple systems for your basic promotional efforts. Any one of your staff should be able to pick up a marketing manual and implement a successful direct mail campaign or place a purposeful advertisement.

Marketing Systems	
Referral program	Regular advertisements
Customer retention program	Advertisement creation system
Regular promotions	Direct mail system
Marketing calendar	Sales procedures
Enquiries management	Lead management

7. Data

While we like to think we operate a paperless office, often the opposite is true. Your business needs to have clear systems for managing paper and electronic information to ensure that information is protected, easily accessed, and only kept when necessary.

Data management systems help you keep your office organized. Everyone knows where information is to be stored, and how it is to be handled, which prevents big stacks of paper with no place to go.

Ensure that within your data management systems you include a data backup system. That way, if anything happens to you server or computer software, your data – and potentially your business – is protected.

Data Management Systems	
IT Management	Client file system
Data backup	Project file system
Computer repairs	Point of sale system
Electronic information storage	Financial data management

Implementing New Systems

If you completed the exercise earlier in this chapter, you will have a good idea of the systems that are currently in place in your business. The next step is to determine what systems you need to create in your business.

To do this you will need to get a better understanding of the tasks that you and your employees complete on a daily and weekly basis. If you operate a timesheet program, this can be a good source of information. Alternately, ask staff to keep a daily log for a week of all the tasks they contribute to or complete. Doing so will not only give you valuable insight into their how they spend their time on a daily basis, but also involve them in the systemizing process.

Review all task logs or timesheet records at the end of the week, remove duplicates, and group like tasks together. From here you can categorize the tasks into business areas like the seven listed above, or create your own categories.

Then, you will need to prioritize and plan your system creation and implementation efforts. Choose one from each category, or one category to focus on at a time. The amount you can take on will depend on your business needs, and the staff resources you have available to you for this process.

Remember that system creation is a long-term process – not something that will transform your business overnight. Be patient, and focus on the items that hold the highest priority.

Creating Your Systems

There is a big variety of ways you can create systems for your business – depending on the type of system you need and the type of business you operate. Some systems will be short and simple – i.e., a laminated sign in the kitchen that outlines step-by-step how to make the coffee – while others will be more complex – i.e., your sales scripts or letter templates.

One thing all of your systems have in common is steps. There is a linear process involved from start to finish. Begin by writing out each of the steps involved in completing the task, and provide as much detail as you can.

Then, review your step-by-step guide with the employee(s) who regularly complete the task and gather their feedback. Once you have incorporated their input, decide what format the system needs to be in: manual, laminated instruction sheet, sign, office memo, etc.

Testing Your Systems

Now that you have created a system, you will need to make sure that it works. More specifically, you need to make sure that it works without your involvement.

Implement the new system for an appropriate period of time – a week or month – then ask for input from staff, suppliers and vendors, and customers. Evaluate if it is informative enough for your staff, seamless enough for your suppliers, and whether or not it meets or exceeds your customer's needs.

Take that feedback and revise the system accordingly. You will rarely get the system right the first time – so be patient.

Systems will also need to be evaluated and revised on a regular basis to ensure your business processes are kept up to date. Structure an annual or bi-annual review of systems, and stick to it.

Employee Buy-In

It will be nearly impossible for you to develop effective systems without the involvement and input of your employees. These are the people who will be using the systems, and who are completing the tasks on a regular basis without systems. They have a wealth of knowledge to assist you in this process.

Employees can also draft the systems for you to review and finalize. This will make the systemization process a much faster and more efficient one.

It is also important to note that when you introduce new systems into your company, there may be a natural resistance to the change. People – including your employees – are habitual people who can become set in the way they are used to doing things.

Delegation

The final step to systemizing your business is delegation. What is the point of creating systems unless someone other than you can use them to perform tasks?

This doesn't have to mean completely removing your involvement from the process, but it does mean giving your employees enough freedom to complete the task within the structure of the systems you have spent time and considerable thought creating.

After that, allow yourself the freedom of focusing on the tasks that you most enjoy, and most deserve your time – like creating big picture strategies to grow your business and increase your profits.

5

How to Create Repeat Business and Have Clients that Pay, Stay and Refer

When it comes to marketing and generating more income, most business owners are focused outward.

They've carefully established and segmented their target market, and created specific offers and messages for each market segment. They spend thousands of dollars in advertising and direct mail campaigns in hot pursuit of more leads, more customers, and more foot traffic.

While this is an effective way to build a business, it is costly and time consuming. It requires constant and consistent effort, and while this approach does generate results, those results quickly disappear when the effort stops or becomes less intense.

Successful businesses that see sustained growth have a double-edged marketing strategy. They focus their efforts *outward* – on new potential customers and marketing – as well as *inward* – on existing customers and referral business.

These successful businesses have leveraged their existing efforts to generate more revenue. Simply put, their customers buy from them over and over again.

For most businesses, this is the easiest way to increase their revenues. Simple customer loyalty strategies and outstanding customer service are often all you need to dramatically increase your sales – from the customers you already have.

The Cost of Your Customers

Do you know how much it costs your business to buy new customers?

Each new customer that walks through your door – with the exception of referrals – has cost you money to acquire. You have spent money on advertising and promotions to generate leads and turn those leads into customers.

For example, if you have placed an ad in your local newspaper for $1,000, and the ad brings in 10 customers, you have paid $100 to acquire each customer. You would need to ensure each of those customers spent at least $200 to cover your margin and break even.

Alternately, if you spent two hours of your time and $10 per month on an email marketing program to send a newsletter to your existing database of customers, and you bring in 10 customers as a result – each customer has cost you $1.

Generating more repeat business means focusing on the marketing strategies that aim to keep your existing customers instead of purchase new ones – effectively reducing the cost of attracting new customers to your business.

These strategies are simple to implement, and don't require much time investment. Just a solid understanding of how to make customers want to come back and spend more of their money

Keeping Your Customers

Marketing strategies that focus on keeping your current customer base are easy and enjoyable to implement. They allow you to build real relationships with the people you do business with, instead of dealing with a revolving door of people on the other end of your sales process.

Repeat customers create a community of people around your business that presumably share the same needs, desires and frustrations. The information you gain from these customers (market research) can help you strengthen your understanding of your target audience, and more accurately segment it.

Remember – 80% of your revenue comes from 20% of your customers. Always focus on these customers. They are ideal customers that you want to recruit, and hold on to.

Customer Service: Make them love buying from you

Every business – even those with excellent service standards can improve the service they provide their customers. Customer service seems to be a dying concept in most businesses; more focus seems to be placed on the speed of the transaction. These days you can even go to the grocery store now and not speak to a single sales associate thanks to self-serve checkouts.

To improve your company's customer service standards, take a survey of your customers and your employees to brainstorm ways you can improve the experience of buying from your business.

Successful customer service standards – those that make your customers *buy* – are:

Consistent. The standards are up kept by every person in your organization. Expectations are clear and followed through. Customers know what to expect, and choose your business because of those expectations.

Convenient. It is nearly effortless for the customer to spend money at your place of business. Convenience can take many forms – location, product selection, value-added services like delivery – and it is also consistent.

Customer-driven. The service the customer receives is exactly how they would like to be treated when buying your product or service. It is reflective of your target market, and appropriate to their lifestyle. Customers would probably not appreciate white linen tablecloths at a fast food restaurant, but they would appreciate a 2-minutes or less guarantee.

Newsletters: Keep in touch with your customers

A regular newsletter is an easy, time-effective, and inexpensive marketing strategy to implement. Unfortunately, many small businesses think these are too time consuming and too expensive to adopt as part of their marketing strategy.

The most popular type of newsletter distribution is email. This will cost your business as little at $10 per month for an email marketing service subscription, and can be customized to your unique branding.

Here is an easy five-step process to starting a company newsletter:

1. **Pick your audience.** New customers? Market segment? Existing customers?
2. **Choose what you're going to say.** Company news? Feature product? New offer?
3. **Determine how you're going to say it.** Articles? Bullet points? Pictures?
4. **Decide how it's going to get to your audience.** Email? Mail? In-store?
5. **Track your results.** How many people opened it? Read it? Took action?

Value Added Service: Give them happy surprises

Adding value to your business is an effective way of getting your customers back. Every person I know would choose a mattress store that offered free delivery over one that did not. It's that simple.

There are many ways to add value to your business, including:

○ **Feature your expertise.** Use your knowledge to provide additional value to your customers. Offer a free consumer guide or report with every purchase.

○ **Add convenience services.** Offer a service that makes their purchase easier, or more convenient. The best example of this is free shipping or delivery.

○ **Package complementary services**. Packaging like items together creates an increase in perceived value. This is great for start-up kits.

○ **Offer new products or services**. Feature top of the line or exclusive products, available only at your business. Offer a new service or profile a new staff member with niche expertise.

Value added services generate repeat customers in one of two ways:

1. **Impress them on their first visit.** Impress you customer with great service, a product that meets their needs, and then wow them with something extra that they weren't expecting. Get them to associate the experience of dealing with your business with happy surprises, and create a perception of higher value.

2. **Entice them to come back.** The introduction of a new value-added service can be enough to convince a customer to buy from you again. Their initial purchase established a trust and knowledge of your business and its processes. They will want to "be included" in anything new you have to offer – especially if there is exclusivity. It is easier to attract clients that have purchased from you than potential clients who have not.

Customer Loyalty Programs: Give them incentives

Another simple way to keep in touch with existing customers and keep them coming back to you is to create a customer loyalty program.

These programs do not have to be complicated or costly, and are relatively easy to maintain once they have been implemented. These programs help you gain more information on your customers and their purchasing habits.

Here are some examples of simple loyalty programs that you can implement:

Free product or service. Give them every 10th (or 6th) product or service free. Produce stamp cards with your logo and contact information on it.

Reward dollars. Give them a certain percentage of their purchase back in money that can only be spent in-store. Produce "funny money" with your logo and brand.

Rewards points. Give them a certain number of points for every dollar they spend. These points can be spent in-store, or on special items you bring in for points only.

Membership amenities. Give members access to VIP amenities that are not available to other customers. Produce member cards or give out member numbers.

Remember that in order for this strategy to work, you and your team have to understand and promote it. The program in itself becomes a product that you sell.

6

Immediate Sales

If you're a business owner, you're also a salesperson.

You've had to sell the bank to get them to loan you your start-up capital. You've had to sell the best employees on why they should work for your business. You've had to convince your business partner, spouse, and friends why your business idea is a good one.

Now you have to repeatedly sell your product or service to your customers.

The ability to sell effectively and efficiently is one every successful business owner has cultivated, and continues to develop. It can be a complicated and time consuming task; one that you will have to continually work on throughout your career in order to be – and stay – successful.

Fortunately, making sales is a step-by-step process that can be learned, customized, and continuously improved. There are a wide range of tools available to help and support your sales efforts.

You don't have to be the most outgoing, enthusiastic person to be successful at sales. You don't even have to be a good public speaker. All you need is an understanding of the basic sales process, and a genuine passion for what you are selling.

Sales 101

As I said before, making sales is a process. There are clear, step-by-step actions that can be taken and result in a sale.

The sales process varies according to the type of business, type of customers and type of product or service that is offered; however, the core steps are the same. Similarly, sales training varies from individual to individual, but the core skills and abilities remain the same.

Here is a basic seven-step process that you can follow, or fine tune to suit your unique products and services. Remember that each step is important, and builds on the step previous. It is essential to become adept at each step, instead of solely focusing on closing the sale.

1. Preparation

Make sure you have prepared for your meeting, presentation, or day on the sales floor. You have complete control of this part of the sales process, so it is important to do everything you can to set the stage for your success.

- Understand your product or service inside and out.
- Prepare all the necessary materials, and organize them neatly.
- Keep your place of business tidy and organized. Reface product on shelves.
- Ensure you appear professional and well groomed.
- Do some research on your potential client and brainstorm to find common ground.

2. Build a Relationship

The first few minutes you spend with a potential customer set the stage for the rest of your interaction. First impressions are everything. Your goal in the second step is to relax the customer and begin to develop a relationship with them. Establishing a real relationship with your customer will create trust.

- Make a great first impression: shake hands, make eye contact, and introduce yourself.
- Remain confident and professional, but also personable.
- Mirror their speech and behavior.
- Begin with general questions and small talk.
- Show interest in them and their place of business.
- Notice and comment on positives.
- Find some common ground on which to relate.

3. Discuss Needs + Wants

Once you have spent a few moments getting to know your prospect, start asking open-ended questions to discover some of their needs and wants. If they have come to you on the sales floor, ask what brought them in the store. If you are meeting them to present your product or service, ask why they are interested in, or what criteria they have in mind for that product or service.

- If you are making a sales presentation, ask for a few moments at the outset to outline the purpose of your visit, as well as how you have structured the presentation.
- Listen intently, and repeat back information you are not sure you understand.
- Ask open-ended questions to get them talking. The longer they talk, the more insight they are providing you into their needs and purchase motivations.
- Ask clarifying questions about their responses.
- If you become sure the customer is going to buy your product or service, begin to ask questions specific to the offering. i.e., what size/color do you prefer?

4. Present the Solution

Once you have a solid understanding of what they are looking for, or what issue they are looking to resolve, you can begin to present the solution: your product or service.

- Explain how your product or service will solve their problem or meeting their needs. If several products apply, begin by presenting the mid-level product.
- Illustrate your points with anecdotes about other happy customers, or awards the product or service has earned.
- Use hypothetical examples featuring your customer. Encourage them to picture a scenario after their purchase.
- Begin by describing the benefits of the product, then follow up with features and advantages.
- Watch your customer's behavior as you speak, and ask further qualifying questions in response to body language and verbal comments.
- Give the customer an opportunity to ask you questions or provide feedback about each product or service after you have described or explained it.
- Ask closed-ended questions to gain agreement.

5. Overcome Objections

As you present the product or service, take note of potential objections by asking open-ended questions and monitoring body language. Expect that objections will arise and prepare for it. Consider brainstorming a list of all potential objections, and writing down your responses.

- Repeat the objection back to the customer to ensure you understand them correctly.
- Empathize with what they have said, and then provide a response that overcomes the objection.

- Confirm that the answer you have provided has overcome their objection by repeating yourself.

The Eight Most Common Objections
The product or service does not seem valuable to me. There is no reason for me to act know. I will wait. It's safest not to make a decision right away. There is not enough money for the purchase. The competitor or another department offers a better product. There are internal issues between people or departments. The relationship with the decision maker is strained. There is an existing contract in place with another business.

6. Close

This is an important part of the sales process that should be handled delicately. Deciding when to close is a judgment call that must be made in the moment during the sale. Ideally, you have presented a solution to their problem, overcome objections, and have the customer in a place where they are ready to buy.

Here are some questions to ask before you close the sale:

- Does my prospect agree that there is value in my product or service?
- Does my prospect understand the features and benefits of the product or service?
- Are there any remaining objections that must be handled?
- What other factors could influence my prospect's decision to buy?
- Have I minimized the risk involved in the purchase, and provided some level of urgency?

Once you have determined it is time to make the sale, here are some sample statements you can use to get the process rolling:

- So, should we get started?
- Shall I grab a new one from the back?
- If you just give me your credit card, I can take care of the transaction while you continue browsing.
- When would you like the product delivered?
- We can begin next month if we receive payment by the end of the week.
- Can I email you a draft contract tomorrow?

7. Service + Follow-up

Once you have made the sale, your work is not over. You want to ensure that that customer will become a loyal, repeat customer, and that they will refer their friends to your business.

Ask them to be in your customer database, and keep in touch with regular newsletters. Follow up with a phone call or drop by to ask how they are enjoying the product or service, and if they have any further questions or needs you can assist them with.

This contact opportunity will also allow you ask for a referral, or an up sell. At the very least, it will ensure you are continuing to foster and build a relationship with the client.

Up selling

Up selling is simply inviting your customers to spend more money in your business by purchasing additional products or services. This could include more of the same product, complementary products, or impulse items.

Regardless, up selling is an effective way to increase profits and create loyal clients – without spending any money to acquire the business. These clients are already purchasing from you – which means they perceive value in what you have to offer – so take the information you have gained in the sales process and offer them a little bit more.

You experience up selling on a daily basis. From "do you want fries with that?" to "have you heard about our product protect program?"

companies across the globe have tapped into and trained their staff on the value of the up sell.

Up selling is truly rooted in good customer service. If your client purchases a new computer printer, you'll need to make sure they have the cords required to connect it to the computer, regular and photo paper, and color and black and white ink.

If you don't suggest these items, they may arrive home and realize they do not have all the materials needed to use the product. They may choose to purchase those materials somewhere closer, cheaper, or more helpful.

Customer education is another form of up selling. What if you customer doesn't realize that you sell a variety of printer paper and stationery in addition to computer hardware like printers? Take every opportunity to educate your customer on the products and services you offer that may be of interest to them.

An effective way of implementing an up sell system into your business is simply by creating add-on checklists for the products or services you offer. Each item has a list of related items that your customer may need. This will encourage your staff to develop the habit of asking for the up sell.

Other up sell strategies can be implemented:

- **At the point of sale**. This is a great place for impulse items like candy, flashlights, nail scissors, etc.

- **In a newsletter**. This is an effective strategy for customer education.

- **In your merchandising**. Place strips of impulse items near related items. For example, paper clips with paper and pens near binders.

- **Over the phone**. If someone is placing an order for delivery, offer additional items in the same shipment for convenience.

- **With new products**. Feature each new product or service that you offer prominently in your business, and ask your staff to mention it to every customer.

Sales Team

Employing a team of strong salespeople

What Makes a Good Salesperson?

There are a lot of salespeople out there – but what qualities and skills make a great salesperson? These are the attributes you will want to find or develop in your team:

- Willingness to continuously learn and improve sales skills
- Sincerity in relating to customers and providing solutions to their objectives
- An understanding of the company's big picture
- A communication style that is direct, polite, and professional
- Honesty and respect for other team members, customers, as well as the competition.
- Ability to manage time
- Enthusiastic
- Inquisitive
- A great listener
- Ability to quickly interpret, analyze, and respond to information during the sales process
- Ability to connect and develop relationships of trust with potential clients
- Professional appearance

Team Building – Keeping Your Team Together

In many businesses, sales is a department or a whole team of people who work together to generate leads and convert customers. Effective management of your sales team is a skill every business owner should cultivate.

Teambuilding, recruitment, and training will be discussed in later sections, but take some time to consider the following aspects of managing a sales team:

Communication
- Are targets and results regularly reviewed?
- Are opportunities for input regularly provided?
- Do sales staff members have a clear understanding of what is expected?
- Do all staff members know daily, weekly, and quarterly targets?

Performance Management
- Are sales staff members motivated to reach targets?
- Are sales staff recognized and rewarded once those targets are reached?
- Are there opportunities for skills training and development?
- Do staff members have broad and comprehensive product or industry knowledge?
- Is there opportunity for growth within the company?
- Is performance regularly reviewed?

Operations
- Do you have a solid understanding of your sales numbers (revenue, profit, margins)?
- Are your sales processes regularly reviewed?
- Do you have a variety of sales scripts prepared?
- Do you measure conversion rates?
- How are your leads generated?

Sales Tools

Every salesperson should have an arsenal of tools on hand to assist them in the sales process. These tools can act as aids while a sale is taking place, or help to foster continual learning and development of the salesperson's skills and approach.

The list below includes some popular sales tools. Add to this list with other resources that are specific to your business or industry.

Tool	Description + Benefit
Scripts	Used for incoming and outgoing telemarketing, cold calls, door-to-door sales, in-store sales Create several different scripts throughout your business Maintains consistency in your sales approach Revise and renew your scripts regularly
Presentation Materials	High-quality information about your product or service Forms: PowerPoint presentation, brochure, product sheets, proposal Serves as an outline of your sales presentation, and keeps you on task
Colleagues	A source of help and advice, especially when you are on the same team or sell similar products Also a source of support
Customer Databases	An accurate, up-to-date database of customer contact information and contact history Used to stay in touch with clients Can also be used for direct mail and follow-up telemarketing

The Internet	A powerful resource for sales help and advice Information to help improve your sales process Online sales coaching Source for product knowledge
Ongoing Training	Constant improvement of your sales skills Constant increase in product knowledge Investment in yourself and your company

8 Tips for Better Sales

- **Dress for the sale.** Dress professionally, appear well put together and maintain good hygiene. Ensure you are not only dressed professionally, but *appropriately*. Would your client feel more comfortable if you wore a suit, or jeans and blazer?

- **Speak their language.** Show you understand their industry or culture, and use phrases your customer understands. This may require researching industry jargon or common phrases. Remember to avoid using words and phrases that are used in the sales process: sold, contract, telemarketing, finance, interest, etc. Doing so will help break down the salesperson/customer barrier.

- **Ooze positivity.** Show up or answer the phone with a smile, and leave your personal or business issues behind. Be enthusiastic about what you have to offer, and how that offering will benefit your customer. Reflect this not only in your voice, but also in your body language.

- **Deliver a strong pitch or presentation**. Be confident and convincing. Leave self-doubt at the door, and walk in assuming the sale. Take time to explain complex concepts, and always connect what you're saying to your audience in a specific way.

- **Be a poster-child for good manners**. Accept any amenity you're offered, listen intently, don't interrupt, don't show up late, have a strong handshake, and give everyone you are speaking to equal attention.

- **Avoid sensitive subjects**. Politics, religion, swearing, sexual innuendos and racial comments are absolutely off-limits. So are negative comments about other customers or the competition.

- **Create a real relationship.** Icebreakers and small talk are not just to pass the time before your presentation. They are how relationships get established. Show genuine interest in everything your customer has to say. Ask questions about topics you know they are passionate. Speak person to person, not salesperson to customer. Remember everything.

- **Know more than you need to.** Impress clients with comprehensive knowledge – not only of your product or service – but also of the people who use that product or service, and industry trends. Been seen as an expert in order to build trust and respect.

7

How to Double
your Referrals

What if I told you that you could put an inexpensive system in place that would effectively allow your business to growth itself?

For most business owners, a large part of their customer base is comprised of referral customers. These people found out about the company's products or services from the recommendation of a friend or colleague who had a positive experience purchasing from that company.

If your business benefits from referral customers, you will find that these customers arrive ready to buy from you, and tend to buy more often. They also tend to be highly loyal to your product or service.

Seem like great customers to have, don't they?

Referral customers cost less to acquire. Compared to the leads you generate from advertising, direct mail campaigns, and other marketing initiatives, referral customers come to you already qualified and already trusting in the quality of your offering and the respectability of your staff.

With a little effort, and the creation of a formalized system – or strategy – you can not only continue to enjoy referral business, but easily double the number of referral customers that walk through your door. All of this is possible for a minimal investment of time and resources.

Is Your Business a Referral Business?

Referral based businesses benefit from a stream of qualified customers who arrive at their doorstep ready to spend. These businesses put less focus on advertising to generate new leads, and more focus on serving and communicating with their existing customers.

Generally speaking, a referral program can generate outstanding results for nearly any business. Since most referrals do not require any effort, the addition of a strategy and a program will often double or triple the number of qualified referrals that come through a business door.

There are, however, a few types of businesses that will not benefit from a formalized referral strategy. These are businesses with low price points – like fast food restaurants and drugstores. Their customer base is large already, and their efforts would be best spent on increasing the average sale.

A referral program can:

- **Save you time**. Referral strategies – once established – don't require much management or time investment.

- **Deliver more qualified customers**. Your customer arrives with an assumption of trust, and willing to purchase.

- **Improve your reputation.** Your customer's networks likely overlap, and create potential for a single customer to be referred by two people. This encourages the perception that your business is "the place to go."

- **Speed the sales process.** You will have existing common ground and a reputation with the referred customer.

- **Increase your profit.** You will spend less time and money generating leads, and more time serving customers who have their wallets open.

The Cost of Your Customers

As we discussed in the "Repeat Business" section, you don't "get" customers, you *buy* them. The money you spend on advertising, direct mail, and other promotions ideally results in potential customers walking through your doors.

For example, if you placed an ad for $200, and 20 people make a purchase in response to that ad, you would have paid $10 for each customer.

Referral customers cost you next to nothing. Your existing customer does the work of selling your business to their friend or associate, and you benefit from the sale. Aside from the cost of any referral incentives or coupon production, there is no cost involved at all.

Referral customers cost less and require less time investment than any other customer. That means you can spend that time making them a loyal customer, or a devoted fan.

Groom Your Customers

Referral strategies can allow you to groom your customer base. As we have previously discussed, 80% of your revenue comes from 20% of your customers – these are your ideal customers.

These are also the people you have established as your target market, and are the people you cater your marketing and advertising efforts toward.

You also have a group of customers who make up 80% of your headaches. These are the people who complain the most and spend the least.

Use your referral strategy to get more of your *ideal* customers. Spend more time servicing your ideal customers – do everything you can to make them happy – and less time on your headache customers. You can even ask your headache customers to shop elsewhere.

Then, focus your referral efforts on your ideal customers. Ask them to refer business to you, and reward them for doing so. Try to avoid referrals from your headache customers – chances are you'll just get another headache.

Referral Sources

Take some time to brainstorm all the people who could potentially refer business to you. Think beyond your business, to your extracurricular activities and personal life. There are endless sources of people who are ready and willing to send potential customers your way.

Here are some ideas to get you started:

Past Relationships

No, not romantic relationships. I'm talking about anyone you have previously had a relationship with, but for one reason or another have fallen out of touch. This includes former colleagues, associates, customers and friends.

Including them in your referral strategy can be as simple as reaching out through the phone or email, and updating them on your latest business initiative or career move. Gently ask at the end of the correspondence to refer anyone who may need your product or service. They will appreciate that you have attempted to re-establish the relationship.

Suppliers and Vendors

Your suppliers and vendors can be a great source for referrals, because they presumably deal daily with businesses that are complementary to your own. The opportunities to connect two of their customers in a mutually beneficial relationship are endless. These businesses should be happy to help out - especially if you have been a regular and loyal customer.

Customers

Customers are an obvious source of referrals because they are the people who are dealing with you directly on a regular basis. Often, all you have to do is ask and they will happily provide you with contact information of other interested buyers, or contact those buyers themselves.

Your customers also have a high level of product knowledge when it comes to your business, and are in a great position to really sell the strength of your company. Remember from the Testimonials section, the words of your customers are at least 10 times more powerful than any clever headline or marketing piece you could create.

Employees and Associates

Give your employees and associates a reason to have their friends and families shop at your business with a simple incentive program. These people have the most product knowledge, and are in the best position to sell you to a potential customer.

This is also a way to tap into an endless network of people. Who do your employees and associates know? Who do their friends and friends of friends know? A referral chain that connects to your employees can be a highly powerful one.

Competitors

This doesn't seem so obvious, but it can work. Your direct competitors are clearly not the ideal source for referrals. However, indirect competitors can refer their clients or potential clients to you if they cannot meet those clients' needs themselves.

For example, if you sell high end lighting fixtures, the low-budget lighting store down the street may be able to refer clients to you, and vice versa. You may wish to offer a finder's fee or incentive to establish this arrangement.

Your Network

Don't be shy about asking your friends and family members for referrals. Too many people do not provide enough information to their inner circle about what they do or what their business does. This doesn't make sense, since these are the people who should be the most interested!

Take time to explain clearly what your business is all about, and what your point of difference is. Then just ask them if they know anyone who may benefit from what you are offering. You could even provide your friends and family with an incentive – a gift, a meal, or a portion of the sale.

Associations + Special Interest Groups

This is another place you likely have a network of people who have limited knowledge about what you do or what your business does. The advantage here is that you have a group of people with similar belief s and values in the same room. Use it!

The Media

Unless a member of the media is a regular customer of yours, or you are in business to serve the media, this may not seem like an obvious choice either.

The opportunity here is to establish a relationship with an editor or journalist, and position yourself as an expert in your field or industry. Then, next time they are writing a related story, they can ask to quote you and your opinion. When their audience reads the story, they will perceive your business as the industry leader.

Referral Strategies

A referral strategy is any system you can put in place to generate new leads through existing customers. The ideal way to do this is to create a system that runs itself! Here are some ideas for simple strategies you can begin to implement into your business immediately.

Just Ask

This may seem simple and obvious, but it's true. Be open with your customers and associates, and simply ask them if they can refer any of their friends or associates to you. Make it part of doing business with you, and your customers will grow to expect the question. Or, let them know in advance that you'll be asking at a later date.

Remember that this can include potential customers – even if they don't buy from you. The reason they chose not to purchase may have nothing to do with your business; any person who has begun to or actually done business with you can refer to you another person.

Offer Incentives

When you speak to your customers, when you ask them for something, you typically try to answer the question "what's in it for me?" before they ask it.

The same is true when you ask your customers for a referral. Incentive-based referral strategies work wonders, and can easily be implemented as part of a customer loyalty program, or as part of your existing customer relations systems.

Consider offering customers who successfully refer clients to you discounts on products, free products or services, or gifts. Offer incentives relative to the number of referrals, or the success rate of each referral.

This can have a spin off effect, as your referral customers may become motivated to continue the referral chain. They too will be interested in the incentives you have provided, and tell their friends about your business.

Be Proactive

The only way your referral program will work is if you put some effort into it, and maintain some level of ongoing effort.

Here are some ideas:

- Put a referral card or coupon in every shopping bag that leaves your store
- Promote gift certificates during peak seasons
- Offer free information seminars to existing customers, and ask them to bring a friend
- Host a closed-door sale for your top 20 customers and their friends

Provide Great Customer Service

An easy way to encourage referral business is to treat every potential customer with exemplary customer service. Since the art of customer service is lost is many communities, people are often impressed by simple added touches and conveniences. That alone will encourage them to refer your business to their network.

Stay in Touch

Make sure you are staying in touch with all of your potential and converted customers. Through newsletters, direct mail, or the Internet, keep your business name at the top of the minds, ahead of the competition.

Even if they have already purchased from you, and may not need to purchase for some time, a newsletter or email can be a simple reminder that your business is out there. If someone in their network is looking for the product or service, it will be more likely that your customer will refer your business over the competition.

8

Generating an Unlimited Amount of Leads for Your Business

Where do your customers come from?

Most people would probably choose advertising as an answer. Or referrals. Or direct mail campaigns. This may seem true, but it's not really accurate.

Your customers come from leads that have been turned into sales. Each customer goes through a two-step process before they arrive with their wallets open. They have been converted from a member of a target market, to a lead, then to a customer.

So, would it not stand to reason then, that when you advertise or send any marketing material out to your target market, that you're not really trying to generate customers? That instead, you're trying to generate leads.

When you look at your marketing campaign from this perspective, the idea of generating leads as compared to customers seems a lot less daunting. The pressure of closing sales is no longer placed on advertisements or brochures.

From this perspective, the **general purpose of your advertising and marketing efforts is then to generate leads from qualified customers.** Seems easy enough, doesn't it?

Where Are Your Leads Coming From?

If I asked you to tell me the top three ways you generate new sales leads, what would you say?

- Advertising?
- Word of mouth?
- Networking?
- ...don't know?

The first step toward increasing your leads is in understanding how many leads you currently get on a regular basis, as well as where they come from. Otherwise, how will you know when you're getting more phone calls or walk-in customers?

If you don't know where your leads come from, start *today.* Start asking every customer that comes through your door, "how did you hear about us?" or "what brought you in today?" Ask every customer that calls where they found your telephone number, or email address. Then, *record the information for at least an entire week.*

When you're finished, take a look at your spreadsheet and write your top three lead generators here:

1. _____

2. _____

3. _____

From Lead to Customer: Conversion Rates

Leads mean nothing to your business unless you convert them into customers. You could get hundreds of leads from a single advertisement, but unless those leads result in purchases, it's been a largely unsuccessful (and costly) campaign.

The ratio of leads (potential customers) to transactions (actual customers) is called your conversion rate. Simply divide the number of customers who actually purchased something by the number of customers who inquired about your product or service, and multiply by 100.

 # transactions / # leads x 100 = % conversion rate

If, in a given week, I have 879 customers come into my store, and 143 of them purchase something, the formula would look like this:

[143 (customers) / 879 (leads)] x 100 = 16.25% conversion rate

What's Your Conversion Rate?

Based on the formula above, you can see that the higher your conversion rate, the more profitable the business.

Your next step is to determine you own current conversion rate. Add up the number of leads you sourced in the last section, and divide that number into the total transactions that took place in the same week.

Write your conversion rate here:

Quality (or Qualified) Leads

Based on our review of conversion rates, we can see that the number of leads you generate means nothing unless those leads are being converted into customers.

So what affects your ability (and the ability of your team) to turn leads into customers? Do you need to improve your scripts? Your product or service? Find a more competitive edge in the marketplace?

Maybe. But the first step toward increasing conversion rates is to evaluate the leads you are currently generating, and make sure those leads are the right ones.

What are Quality Leads?

Potential customers are potential customers, right? Anyone who walks into your store or picks up the phone to call your business could be convinced to purchase from you, right? Not necessarily, but this is a common assumption most business owners make.

Quality leads are the people who are the most likely to buy your product or service. They are the qualified buyers who comprise your target market. Anyone might walk in off the street to browse a furniture store – regardless of whether or not they are in the market for a new couch or bed frame. This lead is solely interested in browsing, and is not likely to be converted to a customer.

A quality lead would be someone looking for a new kitchen table, and who specifically drove to that same furniture because a friend had raved about the service they received that month. **These are the kinds of leads you need to focus on generating.**

How Do You Get Quality Leads?

- **Know your target market**. Get a handle on who your customers are – the people who are most likely to buy your product or service. Know their age, sex, income, and purchase motivations. From that information you can determine how best to reach your specific audience.

- **Focus on the 80/20 rule.** A common statistic in business is that 80% of your revenue comes from 20% of your customers. These are your star clients, or your ideal clients. These are the clients you should focus your efforts on recruiting. This is the easiest way to grow your business and your income.

- **Get specific.** Focus not only on who you want to attract, but how you're going to attract them. If you're trying to generate leads from a specific market segment, craft a unique offer to get their attention.

- **Be proactive**. Once you've generated a slew of leads, make sure you have the resources to follow up on them. Be diligent and aggressive, and follow up in a timely manner. You've done to work to get them, now reel them in.

Get More Leads from Your Existing Strategies

Increasing your lead generation doesn't necessarily mean diving in and implementing an expensive array of new marketing strategies. Marketing and customer outreach for the purpose of lead generation can be inexpensive, and bring a high return on investment.

You are likely already implementing many of these strategies. With a little tweaking or refinement, you can easily double your leads, and ensure they are more qualified.

Here are some popular ways to generate quality leads:

Direct Mail to Your Ideal Customers

Direct mail is one of the fastest and most effective ways to generate leads that will build your business. It's a simple strategy – in fact, you're probably already reaching out to potential clients through direct mail letters with enticing offers.

The secret to doubling your results is to craft your direct mail campaigns specifically for a highly targeted audience of your *ideal* customers.

Your ideal customers are the people who will buy the most of your products or services. They are the customers who will buy from you over and over again, and refer your business to their friends. They are the group of 20% of your clients who make up 80% of your revenue.

Identify your ideal customers

Who are your ideal customers? What is their age, sex, income, location and purchase motivation? Where do they live? How do they spend their money? Be as specific as possible.

Once you have identified who your ideal customers are, you can begin to determine how you can go about reaching them. Will you mail to households or apartment buildings? Families or retirees? Direct mail lists are available for purchase from a wide range of companies, and can be segregated into a variety of demographic and sociographic categories.

Craft a special offer

Create an offer that's too good to refuse – not for your entire target market, but for your ideal customer. How can you cater to their unique needs and wants? What will be irresistible for them?

For example, if you operate a furniture store, your target market is a broad range of people. However, if you are targeting young families, your offer will be much different than one you may craft for empty-nesters.

Court them for their business

Don't stop at a single mail-out. Sometimes people will throw your letter away two or three times before they are motivated to act. Treat your direct mail campaign like a courtship, and understand that it will happen over time.

First send a letter introducing yourself, and your irresistible offer. Then follow up on a monthly basis with additional letters, newsletters, offers, or flyers. Repetition and reinforcement of your presence is how your customer will go from saying, "who is this company" to "I buy from this company."

Advertise for lead generation

Statistics show that nearly 50% of all purchase decisions are motivated by advertising. It can also be a relatively cost effective way of generating leads.

We've already discussed the importance of ensuring your advertisements are purpose-focused. The general purpose of most advertisements is to increase sales – which starts with leads. However ads that are created solely for lead generation – that is, to get the customers to pick up the phone or walk in the store – are a category of their own.

Lead generation ads are simply designed and create a sense of curiosity or mystery. Often, they feature an almost unbelievable offer. Their purpose is not to convince the customer to buy, but to contact the business for more information.

As always, when you are targeting your ideal audience, you'll need to ensure that your ads are placed prominently in publications that audience reads. This doesn't mean you have to fork over the cash for expensive display ads. Inexpensive advertising in e-mail newsletters, classifieds, and the yellow pages are very effective for lead generation.

Here are some tips for lead generation advertising:

Leverage low-cost advertising

Place ads in the yellow pages, classifieds section, e-mail newsletters, and online. If your target audience is technology savvy, consider new forms of advertising like Facebook and Google Adwords.

Spark curiosity

Don't give them all the information they need to make a decision. Ask them to contact you for the full story, or the complete details of the seemingly outrageous offer.

Grab them with a killer headline

Like all advertising, a compelling headline is essential. Focus on the greatest benefits to the customer, or feature an unbelievable offer.

Referrals and host beneficiary relationships

A referral system is one of the most profitable systems you can create in your business. The beauty is once it's set up, it often runs itself.

Customers that come to you through referrals are often your "ideal customers." They are already trusting and willing to buy. This is one of the most cost-effective methods of generating new business, and is often the most profitable. These referral clients will buy more, faster, and refer further business to your company.

Referrals naturally happen without much effort for reputable businesses, but with a proactive referral strategy you'll certainly double or triple your referrals. Sometimes, you just need to ask!

Here are some easy strategies you can begin to implement today:

Referral incentives

Give your customers a reason to refer business to you. Reward them with discounts, gifts, or free service in exchange for a successful referral.

Referral program

Offer new customers a free product or service to get them in the door. Then, at the end of the transaction, give them three more 'coupons' for the same free product or service that they can give to their friends. Do the same with their friends. This ongoing program will bring you more business than you can imagine.

Host-beneficiary relationships

Forge alliances with non-competitive companies who target your ideal customers. Create cross-promotion and cross-referral direct mail campaigns that benefit both businesses.

Lead Management Systems

Once your lead generation strategies are in place, you'll also need a system to manage incoming inquiries. You'll need to ensure you receive enough information from each lead to follow up on at a later date. You'll also need to create a system to organize that information, and track the lead as it is converted into a sale.

Gathering Information from Your Leads

Here is a list of information you should gather from your leads. This list can be customized to the needs of your business, and the type of information you can realistically ask for from your potential customers.

- Company Name
- Name of Contact
- Alternate Contact Person
- Mailing Address
- Phone Number
- Fax Number
- Cell Phone
- Email Address
- Website Address
- Product of Interest
- Other Competitors Engage

Lead List Management Methods:

Once you have gathered information from your lead, you'll need a system to organize their information and keep a detailed contact history.

The simplest way to do this is with a database program, but you can also use a variety of hard copy methods.

Electronic Database Programs

- High level of organization available
- Unlimited space for notes and record-keeping
- Data-entry required
- Examples include: MS Outlook, MS Excel, Maximizer
- Customer Relationship Management Software

Index Cards

- Variety of sizes: 3x5, 4X6 or 5X8
- Basic contact information on one side
- Notes on the other side
- Easy to organize and sort

Rolodex System

- Maintain more contacts than index card system
- Easily organized and compact
- Basic contact information on one side
- Notes on the other side
- Can keep phone conversation and purchase details

Notebook

- Best if leads are managed by a single person
- Lots of room for notes
- Inexpensive
- Difficult to re-organize

- Best for smaller lists

Business Card Organizer

- Best for small lists – under 100
- Limited space for notes
- No data entry required
- Rolodex-style, or clear binder pages

9

Use Goal Setting Effectively

We've all heard about the power of setting goals. Everyone has surely seen statistics that connect goal setting to success in both your business life, and your personal life. I'm sure if I asked you today what your goals are, you could rattle off a few wants and hopes without thinking too long.

However, what most people do not realize is that the power of goal setting lies in *writing goals down*. Committing goals to paper and reviewing them regularly gives you a 95% higher chance of achieving your desired outcomes. Studies have shown that only three to five percent of people in the world have written goals – the same three to five percent who have achieve success in business and earn considerable wealth.

These studies have also found that by retirement, only four per cent of people in the world will have enough accumulated wealth to maintain their income level, and quality of life. As a business owner, it is essential that you develop a plan for your retirement, but it is equally essential that you develop a plan for your success.

This chapter focuses on the power of goal setting as part of your business success. We'll teach you to set SMART goals that are rooted in your own personal value system, and supporting techniques to achieve your goals faster.

What are Goals?

Goals are clear targets that are attached to a specific time frame and action plan; they focus your efforts, and drive your motivation in a clear direction. Goals are different from dreams in that they outline a plan of action, while dreams are a conceptual vision of your wish or desired outcome.

Goals require work; work on yourself, work for your business, and work for others. You cannot achieve a goal – no matter how badly you want it – without being prepared to make a considerable effort. If you are ready to invest your time and energy, goals will help you to:

- Realize a dream or wish for your personal or business life
- Make a change in your life – add positive, or remove negative
- Improve your skills and performance ability
- Start or change a habit – positive or negative

Why Set Goals?

As we've already reviewed, setting goals and committing them to paper is the most effective way to cultivate success. The most important reason to set a goal is **to attach a clear action plan to a desired outcome.**

Goals help focus our time and energy on one (or several) key outcome at a time. Many business owners have hundreds of ideas whirring around in their heads at any one time, on top of daily responsibilities. By writing down and focusing on a few ideas at a time, you can prioritize and concentrate your efforts, avoid being stretched too thin, and produce greater results.

Since goals attach action to outcomes, goals can help to break down big dreams into manageable (and achievable) sections. Creating a multi-goal strategy will put a road map in place to help you get to your desired outcome. If your goal is to start a pizza business and make six figures a year, there are a number of smaller steps to achieve before you achieve your end result.

Success doesn't happen by itself. It is the result of consistent and committed action by an individual who is driven to achieve something. Success means something different for everyone, so creating goals is a personal endeavor. Goals can be large and small, personal and public, financial and spiritual. It is not the size of the goal that matters; what matters is that you write the goal down and commit to making the effort required to achieve it.

What happens when I achieve a goal?

You should congratulate yourself and your team, of course! By rewarding yourself and your team after every achievement, you not only train your mind to associate hard work with reward, but develop loyalty among your employees.

You should also ask yourself if your achievement can be taken to the next level, or if your goal can be stretched by building on the effort you have already made. Consistently setting new and higher targets will lay the framework for constant improvement and personal and professional growth.

Power of Positive Thinking

When was the last time you tuned into your internal stream of consciousness? What does the stream of thoughts that run through your mind sound like? Are they positive? Negative? Are they logical? Reasonable?

Positive thinking and healthy self-talk are the most important business tools you can ever cultivate; by programming a positive stream of subconscious thoughts into your mind, you can control your reality, and ultimately your goals. Think about someone you know who is constantly negative; someone who complains and whines and makes excuses for their unhappiness. How successful are they? How do their fears and doubts become reality in their world?

You are what you continuously believe about yourself and your environment. If you focus your mind on something in your mental world, it will nearly always manifest as reality in your physical world.

Positive thinking is a key part of setting goals. You won't achieve your goal until you believe that you can. You will achieve your goals faster when you believe in yourself, and the people around you who are helping to make your goal a reality.

Successful people are rooted in a strong belief system – belief in themselves, belief in the work they are doing, and belief in the people around them. They are motivated to improve and learn, but also confident in their existing skills and knowledge. Their positive attitude and energy is clearly felt in everything they do.

Ever notice how complainers usually surround themselves with other complainers? The same is true of positive thinkers. If you cultivate an upbeat and positive attitude, you will be surrounded by people who share your values and outlook on life.

Too often, people and our society subscribe to a continuous stream of negative chatter. The more you hear it, the more you'll believe it.

How many times have you heard:

- That's impossible.
- Don't even bother.
- It's already been done.
- We tried that, and it didn't work.
- You're too young.
- You're too old.
- You'll never get there.
- You'll never get that done.
- You can't do that.

Positive thinking and positive influences will provide the support you need to achieve your goals. Choose your friends and close colleagues wisely, and surround yourself with positive thinkers.

Creating SMART Goals

SMART goals are just that: smart. Whether you are setting goals for your personal life, your business, or with your employees, goals that have been developed with the SMART principle have a higher probability of being achieved.

The SMART Principle

1. Specific

Specific goals are clearer and easier to achieve than nonspecific goals. When writing down your goal, ask yourself the five "W" questions to narrow in on what exactly you are aiming for. Who? Where? What? When? Why?

For example, instead of a nonspecific goal like, "get in shape for the summer," a specific goal would be, "go to the gym three times a week and eat twice as many vegetables."

2. Measurable

If you can't measure your goal, how will you know when you've achieved it? Measurable goals help you clearly see where you are, and where you want to be. You can see change happen as it happens.

Measurable goals can also be broken down and managed in smaller pieces. They make it easier to create an action plan or identify the steps required to achieve your goal. You can track your progress, revise your plan, and celebrate each small achievement. For example, instead of aiming to increase revenue in 2009, you can set out to increase revenue by 30% in the next 12 months, and celebrate each 10% along the way.

3. Achievable

Goals that are achievable have a higher chance of being realized. While it is important to think big, and dream big, too often people set goals that are simply beyond their capabilities and wind up disappointed. Goals can stretch you, but they should always be feasible to maintain your motivation and commitment.

For example, if you want to complete your first triathlon but you've never run a mile in your life, you would be setting a goal that was beyond your current capabilities. If you decided instead to train for a five mile race in six months, you would be setting an achievable goal.

4. Relevant

Relevant – or realistic – goals are goals that have a logical place in your life or your overall business strategy. The goal's action plan can be reasonably integrated into your life, with a realistic amount of effort.

For example, if your goal is to train to climb to base camp at Mount Everest within one year and you're about to launch a start-up business, you may need to question the relevance of your goal in the context of your current commitments.

5. Timely

It is essential for every goal to be attached to a time-frame – otherwise it is merely a dream. Check in to make sure that your time-frame is realistic - not too short, or too long. This will keep you motivated and committed to your action plan, and allow you track your progress.

Autosuggestion + Visualization

Autosuggestion and visualization are two techniques that can assist you in achieving your goals. Some of the most well-known and successful people in the world use these techniques, and it is not coincidence that they are masters in their own fields of business and sport. A few of these people include:

- Michael Phelps (Olympic Swimmer)
- Andre Agassi (Tennis)
- Donald Trump (Real Estate)
- Wayne Gretzky (Hockey)
- Bill Gates (Microsoft)
- Walt Disney (Entertainment)

Of course, each of these people have a high degree of talent, ambition, intelligence and drive. However, to reach the top of their respective field, they have each used Autosuggestion and Visualization.

Autosuggestion

Autosuggestion is your internal dialogue; the constant stream of thoughts and comments that flows through your mind, and impacts what you think about yourself and how you perceive situations.

Since you were a small child, this self-talk has been influenced by your experiences and has programmed your mind to think and react in certain ways. The good news is that you can reprogram your mind and customize your self-talk any way you like. That is the power of Autosuggestion.

To begin practicing Autosuggestion, make sure you are relaxed and open to trying the technique; an ideal time is just before bed, or when you have some time to sit quietly. Then, repeat positive affirmations to yourself about the ideal outcome. Top sports and business people will often practice just before a big game or meeting.

Some examples of positive self-talk or autosuggestion include:

- I will lead my team to a victory tonight!
- I will be relaxed open to meeting new people at the party tonight!
- I will deliver a clear and impacting speech!

- I will stop worrying and tackle this problem tomorrow!
- I will stand up for my own ideas in the meeting!
- I will remember everything I have studied for the test tomorrow!

Visualization

Visualization is a practice complementary to Autosuggestion. While you can repeat affirmations to yourself over and over, combining this practice with visualization is twice as powerful.

Visualization is exactly what it sounds like: repeatedly visualizing how something is going to happen in your mind's eye. Nearly everyone in sports practices this technique. It has been proven to enhance performance better than practice alone.

This technique can easily be applied to business. For example, prior to any presentation or meeting where you must speak, present or "perform." You can also visualize yourself being incredibly productive and effective in your office. Or, having a discussion with your spouse calmly and rationally.

Elements to think about during visualization:

- What does the room look like?
- What do the people in the room look like?
- What is their mood? How do they receive me?
- What image do I project?
- How do I look?
- How do I behave? What is my attitude?
- What is the outcome?

10

Define Your Target Market

What is a Target Market?

Many businesses can't answer the question: *Who is your target market?* They have often made the fatal assumption that *everyone* will want to purchase their product or service with the right marketing strategy.

A target market is simply the group of customers or clients who will purchase a specific product or service. This group of people all have something in common, often age, gender, hobbies, or location.

Your target market, then, are the people who will buy your offering. This includes both existing and potential customers, all of whom are motivated to do one of three things:

- Fulfill a need
- Solve a problem
- Satisfy a desire

To build, maintain, and grow your business, you need to know who your customers are, what they do, what they like, and why they would buy your product or service. Getting this wrong – or not taking the time to get it right – will cost you time, money, and potentially the success of your business.

The Importance of Knowing Your Target Market

Knowledge and understanding of your target market is the keystone in the arch of your business. Without it, your product or service positioning, pricing, marketing strategy, and eventually, your business could very quickly fall apart.

If you don't intimately know your target market, you run the risk of making mistakes when it comes to establishing pricing, product mix, or service packages. Your marketing strategy will lack direction, and produce mediocre results at best. Even if your marketing message and unique selling proposition (USP) are clear, and your brochure is perfectly designed, it means nothing unless it arrives in the hands (or ears) of the right people.

Determining your target market takes time and careful diligence. While it often starts with a best guess, assumptions cannot be relied on and research is required to confirm original ideas. Your target market is not always your ideal market.

Once you build an understanding of who your target market is, keep up with your market research. Having your finger on the pulse of their motivations and drivers – which naturally change – will help you to anticipate needs or wants and evolve your business.

Types of Markets

Consumer

The Consumer Market includes those general consumers who buy products and services for personal use, or for use by family and friends. This is the market category you or I fall into when we're shopping for groceries or clothes, seeing a movie in the theatre, or going out for lunch. Retailers focus on this market category when marketing their goods or services.

Institutional

The Institutional Market serves society and provides products or services for the benefit of society. This includes hospitals, non-profit organizations, government organizations, schools and universities. Members of the Institutional Market purchase products to use in the provision of services to people in their care.

Business to Business (B2B)

The B2B Market is just what it seems to be: businesses that purchase the products and services of other business to run their operations. These purchases can include products that are used to manufacture other products (raw or technical), products that are needed for daily operations (such as office supplies), or services (such as accounting, shredding, and legal).

Reseller

This market can also be called the "Intermediary Market" because it consists of businesses that act as channels for goods and services between other markets. Goods are purchased and sold for a profit – without any alterations. Members of this market include wholesalers, retailers, resellers, and distributors.

Determining Your Target Market

Product / Service Investigation

The process for determining your target market starts by examining exactly what your offering is, and what the average customer's motivation for purchasing it is. Start by answering the following questions:

Does your offering meet a basic need?	
Does your offering serve a particular want?	
Does your offering fulfill a desire?	
What is the lifecycle of your product / service?	
What is the availability of your offering?	
What is the cost of the average customer's purchase?	
What is the lifecycle of your offering?	
How many times or how often will customers purchase your offering?	
Do you foresee any upcoming changes in your industry or region that may affect the sale of your offering (positive/ negative)?	

Market Investigation

- **On the ground.** Spend some time on the ground researching who your target market might be. If you're thinking about opening a coffee shop, hang out in the neighborhood at different times of the day to get a sense of the people who live, work, and play in the neighborhood. Notice their age, gender, clothing, and any other indications of income and activities.

- **At the competition.** Who is your direct competitor targeting? Is there a small niche that is being missed? Observing the clientele of your competition can help to build understanding of your target market, regardless of whether it is the same or opposite. For example, if you own a children's clothing boutique and the majority of middle-class mothers shop at the local department store, you may wish to focus on higher-income families as your target market.

- **Online.** Many cities and towns – or at least regions – have demographic information available online. Research the ages, incomes, occupations, and other key pieces of information about the people who live in the area you operate your business. From this data, you will gain an understanding of the size of your total potential market.

- **With existing customers.** Talk to your existing customers through focus groups or surveys. This is a great way to gather demographic and behavioral information, as well as genuine feedback about product or service quality and other information that will be useful in a business or marketing strategy.

Who is Your Market?

Based on your product / service and market investigations, you will be able to piece together a basic picture of your target market, and some of their general characteristics. Record some notes here. At this point, you may wish to be as specific as possible, or maintain some generalities. You can further segment your market in the next section.

Consumer Target Market Framework

Market Type:	Consumer	
Gender:	☐ Male	☐ Female
Age Range:		
Purchase Motivation:	☐ Meet a Need ☐ Serve a Want ☐ Fulfill a Desire	
Activities:		
Income Range:		
Marital Status:		
Location:	☐ Neighborhood ☐ Region	☐ City ☐ Country
Other Notes:		

Institutional Target Market Framework

Market Type:	Institutional	
Institution Type:	☐ Hospital ☐ School ☐ Charity ☐ Church	☐ Non-profit ☐ University ☐ Government
Purchase Motivation:	☐ Operational Need ☐ Client Want ☐ Client Desire	
Purpose of Institution:		
Institution's Client Base:		
Size:		
Location:	☐ Neighborhood ☐ Region	☐ City ☐ Country
Other Notes:		

B2B Target Market Framework

Market Type:	Business to Business (B2B)
Company Size:	
Number of Employees:	
Purchase Motivation:	☐ Operations Need ☐ Strategy ☐ Functionality
Annual Revenue:	
Industry:	
Location(s):	
Purpose of Business:	
People, Culture & Values:	
Other Notes:	

Reseller Target Market Framework

Market Type:	Reseller
Industry:	
Client Base:	
Purchase Motivation:	☐ Operations Need ☐ Client Wants ☐ Functionality
Annual Revenue:	
Age:	
Location:	☐ Neighborhood ☐ City ☐ Region ☐ Country
Other Notes:	

Your Target Market: Putting It Together

Based on the information you gather from your product / service and market investigations, you should have a clear vision of your realistic target market. Here are a few examples of how this information is put together and conclusions are drawn:

Target Market Sample 1: Consumer Market

Business: Baby Clothing Boutique	**Business Purpose:**
Market Type: Consumer	- *Meet a need* (provide clothing for infants and children aged 0 to 5 years)
Gender: Women	- *Serve a want* (clothing is brand name only, and has a higher price point than the competition)
Marital Status: Married	
Market Observations: - located on Main Street of Anytown, a street that is seeing many new boutiques open up, proximate to the main shopping mall two blocks from popular mid-range restaurant that is busy at lunch	**Industry Predictions:** - large number of new housing developments in the city and surrounding areas - two new schools in construction - expect to see an influx of new families move to town from Anycity
Competition Observations: - baby clothing also available at two local department stores, and one second-hand shop on opposite side of town	**Online Research:** - half of Anytown's population is female, and 25% have children under the age of 15 years - Anytown's population is expected to increase by 32% within three years - The average household income for Anytown is $75,000 annually

TARGET MARKET: The target market can then be described as married mothers with children under five years old, between the ages of 25 and 45, who have recently moved to Anytown from Anycity, and have a household income of at least $100K annually.

Target Market Sample 2: B2B Market

Business: Confidential Paper Shredding	**Target Business Size:** Small to medium
Market Type: B2B (Business to Business)	**Target Business Revenue:** $500K to $1M
Business Purpose: - *Meet an operations need* (provide confidential on-site shredding services for business documents)	**Target Business Type:** - produce or handle a variety of sensitive paper documentation - accountants, lawyers, real estate agents, etc.
Market Observations: - there are two main areas of office buildings and industrial warehouses in Anycity - three more office towers are being constructed, and will be completed this year	**Industry Predictions:** - the professional sector is seeing revenue growth of 24% over last year, which indicates increased client billing and staff recruitment
- **Competition Observations:** - one confidential shredding company serves the region, covering Anycity and the surrounding towns - provide regular (weekly or biweekly) service, but does not have the capacity to handle large volumes at one time	**Online Research:** - Anycity's biggest employment sectors are: manufacturing, tourism, food services, and professional services

TARGET MARKET:
The target market can then be described as small to medium sized businesses in the professional sector with an annual revenue of $500K to $1M who require both regular and infrequent large volume paper shredding services.

Segmenting Your Market

Your market segments are the groups within your target market – broken down by a determinant in one of the following four categories:

- Demographics
- Psychographics
- Geographics
- Behaviors

Segmenting your target market into several more specific groups allows you to further tailor your marketing campaign and more specifically position your product or service. You may wish to divide your ad campaign into four sections, and target four specific markets with messages that will most resonate with the audience.

For example, the baby clothing store may choose to segment its target market by psychographics, or lifestyle. If the larger target market is *married females with children under five, between the ages of 25 and 45, who have a household income of at least $100K annually*, it can be broken down into the following lifestyle segments:

- Fitness-oriented mothers
- Career-oriented mothers
- New mothers

With these three categories, unique marketing messages can be created that speak to the hot-buttons of each segment. The more accurate and specific you can make communications with your target market, the greater impact you will have on your revenues.

Market Segmentation Variables

Demographic	Psychographic	Geographic	Behavioristic
Age	Personality	Region	Brand Loyalty
Income	Lifestyle	Country	Product Usage
Gender	Values	City	Purchase Frequency
Generation	Attitude	Area	Profitability
Nationality	Motivation	Neighborhood	Readiness to Buy
Ethnicity	Activities	Density	User Status
Marital Status	Interests	Climate	
Family Size			
Occupation			
Religion			
Language			
Education			
Employment Type			
Housing Type			
Housing Ownership			
Political Affiliation			

Understanding Your Target Market

Once you have determined who your market is, make a point of learning everything you can about them. You need to have a strong understanding of who they are, what they like, where they shop, why they buy, and how they spend their time. Remind yourself that you may *think* you know your market, but until you have verified the information, you'll be driving your marketing strategy blind.

Also be aware that markets change, just like people. Just because you knew your market when you started your business 10 years ago, doesn't mean you know it now. Regular market research is part of any successful business plan, and a great habit to start.

Types of Market Research

Surveys

The simplest way to gather information from your clients or target market is through a survey. You can craft a questionnaire full of questions about your product, service, market demographics, buyer motivations, and so on. Plus, anonymous surveys will produce the most accurate information since names are not attached to the results or specific comments.

Depending on the purpose—whether it is to gather demographic information, product or service feedback, or other data—there are a number of ways to administer a survey.

1. Telephone

Telephone surveys are a more time-consuming option, but have the benefit of live communication with your target market. Generally, it is best to have a third party conduct this type of survey to gather the most honest feedback. This is the method that market researchers use for polling, which is highly reliable.

2. Online

Online surveys are the easiest to administer yourself. There a many web-based services that quickly and easily allow to you custom create your survey, and send it to your email marketing list. These services can also analyze, summarize and interpret the results on your behalf. Keep in mind that the results include only those who are motivated to respond, which may slant your results.

3. Paper-based.

Paper surveys are seldom used, and can prove to be an inefficient method. Like online surveys, your results are based on the feedback of those who were motivated for one reason or another to respond. However, the time and effort involved in taking the survey, filing it out, and returning it to your place of business may deter people from participating.

Keep in mind that surveys can be complex to administer, and consume more time and resources than you have planned. If you have the budget, consider hiring a professional market research firm to lead or assist with the process. This will also ensure that the methodology is standard practice, and will garner the most accurate results.

Website Analysis

Tracking your website traffic is an excellent way to research your existing and potential customer's interests and behavior. From this information, you can ensure the design, structure and content of your website is catering to the people who use it – and the people you want to use it.

User-friendly website traffic analytics programs can easily show you who is visiting your site, where they are from, and what pages of your site they are viewing. Services like Google Analytics can tell you what page they arrive at, where they click to, how much time they spend on each page, and on which page they leave the site.

This is powerful (and free!) information to have in your market research, and easy to monitor monthly or weekly, depending on the needs of your business.

Customer Purchase Data (Consumer Behavior)

If you do not have the budget to conduct your own professional market research, you can use existing resources on consumer behavior. While this data may not be specific to your region or city, general consumer research is actual data that can be helpful in confirming assumptions you may have made about your target market.

Your customer loyalty program or Point of Sale system may also be of help in tracking customer purchases and identifying trends in purchase behavior. If you can track who is buying, what they're buying and how often they're buying, you'll have an arsenal of powerful insight into your existing client base.

Focus Groups

Focus groups look at the psychographic and behavioristic aspects of your target market. Groups of six to 12 people are gathered and asked general and specific questions about their purchase motivations and behaviors. These questions could relate to your business in particular, or to the general industry.

Focus group sessions can also be time consuming to organize and facilitate, so consider hiring the services of a professional market research firm. You may also receive more honest information if a third party is asking the questions, and receiving the responses from focus group participants.

For cost savings, consider partnering with an associate in the same industry who is not a direct competitor, and who would benefit from the same market data.

So What Do You Do From Here?

Use this book as direction to start and or enhance the speed of your business success. If you are not as accomplished as you would like to be then the smartest thing to do is...

A) Accept and encourage "Change" as part of your life
B) Focus on what makes you "Successful" more than what makes you busy
C) Remain "Positive" - your life begins today forward ....

Concentrate on strategies to LEARN and the EARN will follow! If you are serious about taking the next step then go to work on yourself, study other business successes, understand marketing strategies and become a sponge for new (proven) material. The amazing thing about the game of business is that when you put proven processes to work and continue to follow them, an abundance of success will follow. The biggest mistake is to start a process and then fallback into your old habits after a short time.

Above all, get the knowledge you need before you step onto the field. Think about it... if you were going to challenge Michael Jordan to a game of H O R S E for money, wouldn't it make sense to learn the game and practice before you stepped on the court to play him? It is amazing to me how many new small business people start the game of business against seasoned professionals (the competition), without first developing the necessary knowledge to be successful. Then they fail and blame the market, the economy, their location, etc.

If you have a business and have not yet managed to start to create wealth and systems that allow you to take time off, build retirement accounts or pay for your children's college, then learn and master the steps outlined in my book. I am a huge advocate of education and mentorships. Get the right information, find someone that knows how to walk you through them and watch your quality of life take new shape.

For a Free Test Drive of all my best tips, tricks and marketing resources, visit https://www.Keys2Business.com.